YOUR STORY MATTERS

VOLUME ONE

AARON JANDA &
19 OTHER AUTHORS

Copyright © 2023 by Legacy Publishing Co.

Legacypublishingco.com

ISBN: 978-0-9966660-2-2

ALL RIGHTS RESERVED. This book contains material protected under International and Federal Copyright Laws and Treaties. Any unauthorized reprint or use of this material is prohibited. No part of this book may be reproduced or transmitted in any form or by any means, electronic or mechanical, including photocopying, recording, and/or by any information storage and retrieval system without express written permission from the Author/Publisher.

Regarding reliability, accuracy, timeliness, usefulness, adequacy, completeness, and/or suitability of information provided in this book, Aaron Janda, Legacy Publishing Co., its partners associates, affiliates, consultants, and/or presenters make no warranties, guarantees, representations, or claims of any kind. You agree that Aaron Janda and/or Legacy Publishing Co. is not responsible for the success or failure of your personal, business, health, or financial decisions relating to any company products/services.

No representation in any part of this information are guarantees or promises of any kind. The Authors and Publisher (Aaron Janda, Legacy Publishing Co. or any representatives) shall in no way, under any circumstances, be held liable to any party (or damages arising directly or indirectly) from any use of books, materials and/or seminar trainings, which are provided "as is" and without warranties.

NKJV - Unless otherwise noted, Scripture references are taken from the New King James Version®. Copyright © 1982 by Thomas Nelson. Used by permission. All rights reserved.

KJV - Scripture quotations from The Authorized (King James) Version. Rights in the Authorized Version in the United Kingdom are vested in the Crown. Reproduced by permission of the Crown's patentee, Cambridge University Press.

NIV / NIVUK - Scripture references are taken from the NEW INTERNATIONAL VERSION. Copyright ©1973, 1978, 1984 International Bible Society. Used by permission of Zondervan Bible Publishers.

ESV - Scripture quotations are from the ESV® Bible (The Holy Bible, English Standard Version®), Copyright © 2001 by Crossway, a publishing ministry of Good News Publishers. Used by permission. All rights reserved.

TPT - Scripture quotations marked TPT are from The Passion Translation®. Copyright © 2017, 2018, 2020 by Passion & Fire Ministries, Inc. Used by permission. All rights reserved. ThePassionTranslation.com.

NLT - Scripture quotations marked NLT are taken from the Holy Bible, New Living Translation, copyright © 1996, 2004, 2007 by Tyndale House Foundation. Used by permission of Tyndale House Publishers, Inc., Carol Stream, Illinois 60188. All rights reserved. http://www.newliving-translation.com/ http://www.tyndale.com

AMP - Scripture quotations taken from the Amplified® Bible Classic, Copyright © 1954, 1958, 1962, 1964, 1965, 1987 by The Lockman Foundation

CONTENTS

Acknowledgments	vii
Introduction Aaron Janda	ix
1. REFUSE TO QUIT Aaron Janda	1
2. I MADE IT! Alexus Main	7
3. I WISH THINGS COULD BE DIFFERENT Kyle Sullivan	17
4. FROM ESPN AND HEARTBREAK TO GOD'S PERFECT PLAN Molly Trotter Gomez	23
5. FROM THE BOOK: BREAKTHROUGH Preston Ducati	29
6. RUN OVER BY A CAR! Charles Chavez	37
7. YOUR LEGACY Sam John	45
8. FROM THE BOOK: STILL STANDING LaToya Andrews	51
9. THE ACCIDENT Joshua Hayes	55
10. THE ROSE THAT GREW FROM CONCRETE Brooke Kelly	63
11. THE DAY I BURNED MY HOUSE DOWN Gary Lunsford	71
12. FROM IRELANDS SHORES Karen Boreland	77
13. LEARNING TO SPEAK AGAIN THROUGH NURSERY RHYMES AND RIGHT-BRAIN ART Darrin Kissinger and Diane Kissinger	85

14. STATE OF SHOCK Jeana Shackelford	93
15. FEAR AND LOVE Bryan Sims	99
16. FINDING PEACE THROUGH TRAUMA Jillian Wilson	105
17. WHY NOT ME? Javier Herrera	111
18. KEEP THE TARGET Thais Guilherme	117
19. FLYING BY FAITH Tina Robinson	127
20. IT'S OK IF YOU'RE NOT THERE YET Katia Motzeva-Gutierrez	133
Conclusion	141
The Invitation	143
About Aaron Janda	147

ACKNOWLEDGMENTS

First, I would like to thank my Lord and Savior, Jesus Christ. Without you pulling me out of the mess of a life that I was living 20+ years ago and never leaving my side for the last 20 years, I am certain I wouldn't be here today without you!

I would also like to thank my family and my closest friends that stayed with me through my successes and my failures! Thank you for being that voice of reason and wisdom in the good times and the bad! Thank you for inspiring me to become the best version of myself and helping me gain clarity and focus to pursue my purpose! Thank you for your encouragement and countless hours of conversations and prayers to propel me forward to where I am today!

And lastly, but definitely not least, I would like to thank every contributor to this Book Project, Your Story Matters! I want to especially thank every individual, every author, every single one of you for trusting me with your stories, your experiences, and your life! Without you, this project wouldn't have been possible! I believe this Book, this Book Series, is going to make an impact beyond what any one of us could have done on our own! We are better together! Now let's go change the world by sharing our stories!

Aaron

INTRODUCTION
AN EXPERIENCE I WILL NEVER FORGET!

AARON JANDA

I want to ask you a question. Have you ever thought about YOUR Story? You're probably thinking, "My Story?" "I don't have a story!" Well, I've found that 100 percent of the people I've met throughout my life have a story of some sort, a story about something they have gone through or experienced, good or bad, that's made them the person they are Today.

I remember an experience, an encounter if you will, that I still think about to this day. In 2009, I was living in Tulsa, Oklahoma, attending college. I was preparing for a one-month internship in the Philippines. I would be teaching in schools, speaking at leadership events, going into prisons to talk with inmates, and donating and delivering food to some of the poorest areas on the Island of Mindinao, PI.

The way my school was set up for the year was that I had to have my entire year's tuition paid in full upfront at enrollment. Because we would have a mandatory one-month internship overseas, we were required to raise the necessary funds to pay for the entire trip, lodging, food, travel, etc., i.e., several thousand dollars. Four to five thousand, to be exact, and we only had a few months to do it.

But that's not the experience I'm thinking of. I remember an encounter I had with a young couple and their small child several months before my trip.

I remember it like it was yesterday. I was standing in the checkout line at a grocery store, before self-checkout was a thing. While I was waiting in line with my groceries, this guy, his girlfriend or wife, and their tiny baby came up behind me. Now, this guy would stand out in a crowd. He was a Hispanic gentleman, covered in tattoos, full sleeves, and tattoos on his neck and face. We were waiting a little longer than usual, so I started making small talk with him, and he introduced himself as "Cowboy."

If the face tatt's, what looked like some jailhouse tatt's, and the nickname didn't give it away, even if he wasn't a gang-banger, I knew that I had to tread carefully with my conversation. So, I did. And we began to talk about my church, with roughly 10,000 plus members not far from the grocery store. And the only reason I mention the size is that the chance of us having any mutual friends or connections would have been slim to none. But we did, the moment I mentioned the church, he immediately asked if I knew a specific person, and I actually did. He was a friend of mine! So, we instantly connected and continued our conversation.

The lady at the checkout started ringing up my groceries, then we began to talk about God. I thought to myself, "Wow! Not the conversation I was expecting!" I paid for my groceries while diving into a deeper conversation with "Cowboy." She proceeds to ring up "Cowboy" and his family's groceries, then suddenly, deep inside my heart, I felt like God said to me, "pay for their groceries from the account with your trip money."

Then the mental gymnastics began. I started this inner dialog between me and God. "But God, that's the money I've been saving for my internship. I need that money!" Then my mind kicked in, "that guy seems like a hard guy. I don't want to embarrass him in front of his girl by paying for his groceries." Then in a split second of obedience, their groceries finished being rung up, the total came on the screen, and I immediately swiped my card!

The cashier quickly reached out for my card, "oh no, sir, that's for their groceries!" "Ding." The transaction went through. Then I thought, "what did I just do?" "This guy might want to fight me!" If you're wondering why he might want to fight me, there is something you have to realize. If you have ever been in a place of "need," it can be extremely humbling to actually receive! As a man with his girl, having another man pay for his groceries can be embarrassing!

Here is where it got interesting, if not even a little sketchy. I was aware of the fact that I might have just embarrassed him. So immediately, I said to him, "hey, you're a friend of so-and-so (our mutual friend), and I felt like God told me to pay for your groceries." We all continued to walk toward the exit. The look on his face told me he was contemplating whether or not to beat the crap out of me. I got very forward with him and addressed the "elephant in the room," I told him, "hey man, I know it can be hard to receive a blessing because it may be humbling or even embarrassing, especially as a man." But I'm telling you that God wants to bless you, and He had me do it just to let you know that He is looking out for you and your family!"

We got out to the parking lot, and I thought this is about to "go down!" But something crazy happened! "Cowboy's" demeanor completely changed, and they both started tearing up. His girlfriend started to cry as she shared that they had been struggling financially. They had gone through their entire grocery list, and every item was accounted for, down to the very dollar that the total came to! At that moment, we all knew that God had created that moment just for them! But even more for myself.

I shared that story to show you the power of stories. Almost every story you hear will have at least one, if not all, of these three elements: emotional connection, relatability, and perspective.

The most influential thought leaders, speakers, and influencers know this! So, without getting into the technical side of public speaking, sharing stories, and connecting with audiences, live or online, I want you to recognize this one thing! Whether it is through books, movies, music, the spoken word, social media, or entertainment as a whole, there is no greater way to connect with someone than through the power of story!

This Book Series, Your Story Matters, is a labor of love for me! This project and the vision of it has been three years in the making. This project was birthed through one of the most difficult seasons of my life these last few years. As I started this project, I began reaching out within my network to people who I knew had some incredible stories to share. Stories of restoration, healing, and redemption. However, most of those outcomes came from the most horrific, devastating, and life-altering experiences. The more stories I heard, the more "perspective" I gained in relation to my own life. No matter how "bad" or traumatic our life experiences have been, there is always someone out there who may have had it worse.

This book is a compilation of some of those stories. As you read this book, I challenge you to not only glean from these stories but also think about your own experiences and your own story!

Please don't fall into the "imposter syndrome" trap that might sound like, "what do I have to offer," "who would want to hear my story," or even "who am I to share my story?" There might be someone out there that needs to hear it, and I'm willing to bet that there most certainly are, and lots of them! As challenging, vulnerable, and scary to share with the world as it may have been, every one of the authors that contributed to this book came to that realization, and they are now sharing it with you!

Remember, YOUR STORY MATTERS!

1

REFUSE TO QUIT

AARON JANDA

"When obstacles arise, you change your direction to reach your goal; you do not change your decision to get there."
-Zig Ziglar

Have you ever felt alone? Have you ever been at a place in your life where you felt like you had nobody to turn to? Have you ever been in a position where you felt like you had no other options? Not too long ago I received news that a friend of mine of 20+ years had taken his own life. I couldn't believe what I was hearing! I had just spoken with him a few months before and we were going to get together and spend some time catching up when I was back in Seattle. He had gone through some pretty hard times, but it sounded like his life had turned around and it was heading in an upward trajectory! I just couldn't wrap my mind around the decision that he had made, however, a few years prior I had gone through some devastating life events of my own, and it clicked! I could relate to the trauma and emotions that may lead someone to a decision like that. I understood being in a place so dark and so alone that one could feel like they had no other options!

I know what it is like to feel alone. Not for a lack of relationships or lack of people being around. But alone, deep down in your soul, a sense of loss or being lost. A lack of direction, hope, and optimism being sucked out of your being. Being the owner of a business yet having no one to discuss its greatest challenges. Being in a relationship or a marriage but feeling alone, alone in purpose, direction, drive, and lack of intimacy. Or quite literally, physically alone, single with no family or children. I've experienced all of those emotions!

Statistically, by the age of thirty-nine, everyone will have at least one polarizing life event that has the potential to either make or break them. I had four of them back-to-back over the course of around a year, and it nearly derailed me and my business career. 2016 was that year for me. I went from being on top of the world one moment to entering one of the darkest seasons of my life the next.

Just a few months earlier, in October 2015, I published my first book, *My $100 Dollar Project*. I felt incredible! I had always wanted to write a book! At the time my first book came together, I was living in Tulsa, Oklahoma but was earning income from a business that I had started several years prior in Seattle. Life was good, my book had done well! I was invited to speak on podcasts as well as the radio, I was planning my book tour, and I was gaining influence in the city because of my book. I was invited to private events and had the privilege of meeting some very influential people in the City of Tulsa because of my book! I remember being on the top of a building at a penthouse Christmas party, dressed to the nines, quite literally feeling like I was on top of the world. Or at least Tulsa!

Then within a few short months, things started to unravel quite rapidly! As I entered 2016, all things concerning my life, marriage, and business would drastically change!

I had a business partner that would go on to steal upwards of $250,000 in royalties. Several months after those payments ceased, I lost a family member to cancer. When I arrived home from that trip to visit my relative right before he passed away, I found that my wife had left me, which would eventually end in divorce. I could not even believe what was happening. My life was completely going off the rails!

I remember coming home after my trip, my wife at the time was gone, yet a strange sense of calm came over me that July evening as I laid down on our bed. I laid there for a while, trying to calculate, figure out, and question the decisions made over the last six months leading up to that point. I looked at other people's choices, decisions, actions, and reactions, as well as my own. Although I had a level of peace and calm, I did have the overwhelming temptation to ask, why me?

A few short months after the separation, I had two lawsuits filed against me by two fortune 500 companies for debts that I couldn't manage because of my previously said business partner. Through this whole process, we accumulated over $120,000 in debt. I was on the verge of bankruptcy, and had very few options!

We cannot control the things that happen to us in this life or the things from our past that may have shaped our negative belief systems. But we can control what we do moving forward!

I titled this chapter, *Refuse To Quit* for a reason! If there is anything that I've learned from my life and experiences, it is this, as long as you refuse to quit, things can get better...way better!! I'm going to be sharing my story in greater detail in my upcoming book, *Refuse To Quit*. However, for the sake of this book, I do only have one chapter, but I won't completely leave you hanging!

I am living proof that as long as you refuse to quit, your life can change in ways that you would never have imagined! Despite all the pressure, anxiety, loss, trauma, or whatever you may be facing, it can be even better than before! I'm not saying it's going to be easy, but I am saying it will be worth it!

I mentioned earlier in the chapter that I knew what it felt like to be alone, lost with a lack of hope, the optimism sucked out of my soul, alone in purpose and direction. After the season I just described to you, I felt a flood of those emotions. I'm going to be honest, I had to traverse through some very dark times and rediscover who I was and what my purpose would be from that moment forward.

I would then go on, over the next few years, to pay off over $120,000 of debt. In 2019 I co-authored two books that would become best-selling books, accomplishing my goal of becoming a best-selling author, now three times over. In 2019 and 2020, I began to develop my current company Legacy Publishing Co. that would end up working with dozens of new and seasoned authors. Empowering them to share their stories like the ones in this book. I began to meet and develop new relationships, and I also realized the relationships that needed to end after reflecting back on the most difficult season of my life. I recently moved back to Seattle, WA, where I'm from. I've been getting more opportunities to speak and share my story with the intention that my life, my experiences, good and bad, may bring hope to someone that might be going through similar, life-altering situations!

I don't know what difficulties you may be experiencing in your life currently or are trying to overcome, but thankfully you are still here! You are reading this book, and hopefully, things are improving for you. As you continue to read the stories in this book, I truly do believe that you will find hope, inspiration, purpose, and direction. As long as you refuse to quit, your life could also make a massive impact on humanity!

I believe in you! Keep going! You are not alone!

2

I MADE IT!

ALEXUS MAIN

I Made It! I'm Alexus, and I MADE IT! Well, I thought I did. You know when you get that feeling of "I AM the BOSS!" I have paved my own way, I'VE MADE IT!" I felt that feeling, walking down the stairs of the second story of the beautiful building at JB Hunt Corporate offices, silently saying goodbye to my corporate salaried job at 10:30 a.m. And when I say silently, I mean I cleared my computer of all the work I had done and packed up all my things in a Walmart sack I had brought my lunch in. I walked passed everyone on my team down the stairs, not saying a SINGLE WORD. I was not even thinking it.

Not until I made it down the stairs and almost out the door, before seeing a friend in the stairwell. I was be-lining for that door for a breath of fresh air like I had just ran 20 miles on a treadmill uphill. She says, "You headed to lunch?" And then, for the first time out loud, I said, "No, I just quit." Of course, no one knew that yet; I feel like I barely knew it yet. This wasn't a decision I had made after thinking about my life and what was best for my family. My family at home... my husband and my two daughters. It was a decision I had made after the phone call with my soon-to-be new boss.

I had an interview with his wife, and I was on their sales call that morning for a job that was like a pipedream for me. He said, "Alexus, you are one of the best natural salespeople at your age that I've seen, but you've never had something that you've never had because you have never done something that you have never done." And that was it. That struck me like a ton of bricks right there in my chair, at my desk, at the job I didn't want. That was the moment I decided to walk out of my job and not tell anyone.

This person I had never met in person, who lived in another state, believed in me. He barely knew me. But he knew about me, something I didn't know. And I was TIRED of being tired. And I ran out that door and went for it. With all of the confidence in the world, I called him right back and said, "I'm ready to hustle. I just quit my job" I remember calling my husband and saying, "Don't freak out, but I just quit my job" He didn't freak out, surprisingly... not yet, anyways.

That first week working from home, I made NO SALES! LIKE ZERO. That was zero money to me. Zero money to my family. The following week my husband was panicking because I made a sale, and it only made me $200, HA! That was not going to get us where we wanted to be, and it was ultimately on me. I was the one that quit my job without even making a plan. I was keeping my head down and working. ME, the girl that quit my corporate job, the girl from the family of all single moms, the girl that got made fun of since kindergarten because of my 'boy' voice (Hey, I'm sure Janis Joplin and I could have had a heck of a duet), I was not about to prove all of the people who told me I could be nothing, RIGHT! And I went for it. ALL IN. That was the only option I had. You don't WALK OUT of your job, and then just go get it back. I burned that bridge. It was gone. It was time to build a new one.

Months went by, and I was rising on the charts on the sales team, going to events, and networking with some of the smartest people I have ever met. I was actually growing and learning, and it was such an 'on fire' feeling! I felt more like myself than I ever had; before that, I didn't know who I was. I wasn't JUST a mom, or JUST a wife, or JUST an employee. I felt so important and valued, and I owned my position. I HAD DONE IT! I had literally transformed my life and actually succeeded when everyone said I couldn't. I was the youngest person on my sales team. I was consistently making five figures a month, and I had a nice car, perfect daughters, and a gorgeous 7-bedroom house! I'm Alexus, and I MADE IT! ...or so I thought.

Have you ever heard someone tell you that the more successful you get or, the more money you have, the more problems you have? Or that money can't change your marriage? Well... friends, it's true. Notice I didn't mention a happy marriage when I listed everything I had.. Unfortunately, it's because I didn't have a happy marriage. I had a marriage, for sure. I was married to my junior high sweetheart, that I had met at a football game in the 8th grade. (aww) I had just moved to a new city and met him, and instantly WE were "IT." When I'm saying I had MADE IT, that's how I felt. My first "I made it!" moment. I had my dream wedding, perfect babies, and I am smart and driven and giving, and I loved being a mom and wife... until I didn't anymore. I worked hard for that life, but something felt so off for some reason. I had been doing it for 10 years. Being in a relationship for 10 YEARS! I was 13 when we met, and we followed that cute little storyline of a wedding, babies, and the whole shindig. However, for me, it just didn't do it. Don't get me wrong, it was great when it was great, but it wasn't when it wasn't. I NEEDED MORE. So many things were missing, and I felt slightly uncomfortable in the little textbook storyline of that 'normal' life. I was programmed to think that was the norm. The marriage stresses and problems. The fights. The crying and lying. I needed more than that. Now I wasn't wanting to be a secret wonder woman and creep through the night saving the good guys and crushing the bad guys. I just wanted to feel ALIVE and on FIRE in every aspect of my life like I did my job!

That's where marriage counseling and then divorce came. It was hard to admit that that wasn't the life I wanted anymore. I wished so badly it was, BUT the more aligned I became with who I wanted to be, the more I realized I loved the idea of marriage and family more than I loved my husband, and I hated it. It wrecked me knowing we didn't go together. CRASH AND BURN. I know; it sucks.

No one passed out manuals at our high school graduation telling you how to handle everything. Much less how to handle it with a 2-year-old and a 4-year-old. We did the "try and fix it thing," but we weren't getting on the same page for so long despite the effort, and it was constant fighting, and it was exhausting. It was hard for me to keep up with everything; unfortunately, it hurt my sales career. Now it's no excuse, but I deserved a little grace. But I got none.

The boss I had, spoke so poorly to his sales team, and he did not like seeing me not making those big numbers. He publicly fired me in a Facebook group of 10's of thousands of people. I woke up to my phone lighting up the entire room like the fourth of July. It was pretty embarrassing, to say the least, and put me in a huge bind. I was sleeping in a different room than my husband, and we were "sharing" the kids. It was a whirlwind in my house.

My husband and I finally got on the same page...the divorce page, and that's not the exact time you want to be unemployed, friends. I won't sit here and act like the divorce was super nasty and horrific. It wasn't. But it was a divorce nonetheless, and they all suck when kids are involved. Add in the no-job thing, and it's a sure-fire recipe for the "greatest" time of your life! I'm kidding, nothing about it is glorious, and I spent many nights crying in the bottom of my closet after my kids were begging for mommy and daddy to live together. That wrecked me.

Did I make It? Heck, I couldn't even make it off the closet floor sometimes. Being a fantastic mom when your heart is breaking, and your life is shattering is the hardest thing I've ever done. Hiding that heartbreak and desperation with smiles and goldfish for a snack. Many days ended in wine on my front porch with my neighbor. We lived in brand-new fourplexes in a brand-new neighborhood across the street from the park, and she knew all about divorce. All my friends had gone through something similar, and they were my pillars. Next to my mom, who I moved in with me for help, those were my people. I had no job, and I hustled up a waitressing job. I could sell anything, so surely I could sell my smile and kindness to my table as a waitress, right?

I was working away, sharing my kids, drinking in my free time, and wondering where I was headed. I had to figure out something QUICK! I went from loving my job and bringing in more money than I ever had to $16 some days. Day shifts were slow, and I was a momma living in a brand-new fourplex, and I couldn't afford those bills on top of that car payment. Waitressing wasn't providing me with that 5-figure a month income I had before.

I was scared and lost, BUT I knew it couldn't be the end. I was made for more. My confidence was beaten down. I had worked so hard TO MAKE IT! My life crashed and burned. I was drinking more than I wanted to be, working more night shifts than I cared to, and facing repossession of my car and probably an eviction notice if I didn't figure it all out. I had to get on food stamps, and life was not looking up for me. That's where I wanted to give up. It got pretty dark. It got dark enough that I felt like my girls would live better without me. Look at me and what I had done. I ripped their whole life apart, and I was crashing and burning. It wasn't my favorite season of my life.

That's where real estate came in. I knew before that I was helping so many people in real estate at my old job, so there was no reason I shouldn't take the knowledge from that job I was fired from and just become a REALTOR! Making it little by little. I was distracted with waitressing, being a mom, trying to keep my head above water, and figuring out how to be ME in such a short 24 hours. It wasn't a Beyonce 24 hours...it was weak and involved alcohol.

Pathetic really. Sometimes when life hits rock bottom, you just want to quit. That class was hard! ESPECIALLY online at home. It took me four times as long to complete the class as it should have. I passed the class, and then I failed the test. I had worked so hard and felt defeated, like I couldn't get it together. I was trying to stay in hustle mode, and it was about to be the holidays, and there was no way I could afford to get my real estate career going and provide Christmas. I was working non-stop with no time to study, just to keep a roof over our heads. I was embarrassed and lost.

Christmas was not in the cards for us, but how do you tell two little girls who just moved into a new house after their mommy and daddy split up that you aren't having Christmas? You don't. Lucky for me, in this dark corner of my life, my very best friends swooped in and provided a beautiful Christmas for my girls. I cried and cried over that, and it hurt so bad knowing I couldn't provide for them.

And in the midst of darkness and chaos came my dream come true. Terrible timing, really. I must have been the queen of that. It was a love I never knew I needed. A love that consumed me and ignited a fire in me I had never felt. The man that knew what I thought before I said it and put me above everything. He completed me. I could feel it. He completed me in this disaster of a life I had. I was so not ready for a fairytale. My life was a wreck. But with him, everything made sense. I was even blending two broken families with two kids each. We felt crazy!

Crazy in love, we were. And we went for it. We had the most beautiful wedding under a lighted tree. I was barefoot in a beautiful dress, and he in his cowboy hat, and it was pure bliss. And boy, did we nail it. I was so happy. My kids were so happy. His kids were so happy. But beneath the surface, I knew I had to keep pushing for ME. I had things that still needed completing. I wanted to slow down and celebrate and love this moment of my life, but I also had a pending Real Estate license that was my goal! And no way did I cry all those tears and lose all those hours of sleep to give up. I pushed it to the last minute, of course. I was so happy I couldn't sit and focus on studying, but everyone around me made me. Ha! They pushed and pushed and forced me not to give up. And after four tests in two weeks, tears, guilt, and anger, I passed... FINALLY! I did it! I was a licensed Arkansas Real Estate Salesperson.

It was the BEGINNING of what I had dreamt of and worked towards. I was thrilled! I met with my broker, learned what I had to do to get going, and yeah... it was expensive! I was still a waitress and a mom of four with a husband who worked the night shift. I got home, and I immediately wanted to cry. Like really life!? Not even ready to give me a break at all? My husband was calm in every storm and was no different then. He forced me to believe that I COULD. That I had made it too far to give up. So, I didn't!

Despite everyone telling me that Realtors quit in their first year and that they need another job during the first year, I quit my job anyways. I knew if I wanted this and didn't want to be one of their statistics, I was all in. And it worked. I got my license at the beginning of February, took my knowledge from my old job, and helped my real estate team for extra cash. In May, I closed four transactions and cleared $11,900.

Do you see that? That broken, divorced, single momma, afraid no one would love her, waitress, cleared ELEVEN THOUSAND DOLLARS. I'm Alexus, and I MADE IT! And this time, I know I did. This time I know that I'm worthy. This time, at that moment when I knew I had made it, it was because I knew myself. I knew I'd never give up. It wasn't the dollar sign that made me feel accomplished. It wasn't the fact that I had nailed this amazing job and smoking hot husband. It was that despite all of the hard things life threw at me, I didn't give up. I didn't quit. I cried on closet floors and drank until I threw up and wanted to quit. Oh, you have no idea how badly I wanted to quit, how part of me wanted to be basic and average, live paycheck to paycheck, and be miserably alone. But I didn't. My people deserved more than that. The people that loved me and believed in me deserved a victory lap.

You see, that little fire inside of me needed fueling. It needed to be put to the test. I needed to feel those temporary failures to push me to where I wanted to be. I needed to use every ounce of me to push through it. So I didn't MAKE it because I got the money and the man. I made it because I did it no matter how dark the darkness and hard the mountain was to climb. I'm in the winner's circle and never plan to leave. There's not a valley I won't walk or a mountain I won't climb to fight for what I want. I know that life is a hell of a pitcher and plenty of curveballs will come my way, but it better be ready for the crack of the bat because I'm Alexus, and I'm ALWAYS going to MAKE IT.

AND YOU CAN TOO!

3

I WISH THINGS COULD BE DIFFERENT

KYLE SULLIVAN

"To wish to change something in the past is to desire to forfeit the lessons learned by going through it."
-Unknown

Take a moment to think about your life up to this point right now. Close your eyes and play the movie of your life starring none other than you. Breathe deep in. Breathe out. Think about the first time you remember laughing until you cried. Think about the first time you remember crying because you experienced hurt. Think about people you couldn't live without and the people you wish you never met. Take a mental picture of all of it.

Now that I have you in a state of awareness and emotions. Let's begin.

The number of people I have heard or read about discussing how they wish they could go back in time to change the past is staggering. I used to believe that if I could be granted a wish to change something in my past, I would do it in a heartbeat. You may be feeling that at this very moment. But I would challenge you to think differently about your past. Let me introduce you to the overview of my story.

My story started in January 1987 when I came into the world to parents that were both still in high school. Within the first few months of my existence, my biological mother would leave my dad and me for reasons still unknown to me at the time of my writing these words. My dad dropped out of high school in his senior year and started working full-time to provide for his new son. With a family to help, my dad worked hard during the first three years of my life to provide for me and him. At three years old, he married the lady I would call "Mom." She is the only person I knew as my mother, and I believed that I was both of theirs biologically. Around middle school, it was revealed that the lady I thought to be my biological mother wasn't. But she was still my mom. However, it put incredible tension in that relationship while I was developing as a pre-teen with more emotions than I knew how to handle. Also, I was a heavier kid for most of my developing years, to the point that my pants didn't have numbers for the waist. It just said "husky."

It's okay, and you can chuckle; I do now too. Who believed that would be good for anyone's self-esteem? Anyway, back to the story.

Because I was a bigger kid, I got picked on and made fun of, but for the most part, I was able to shake it off, but the wounds mentally would stick around for much longer than I care to admit. I had to figure out ways to deflect and distract myself and others from making fun of me, so I became obsessed with sports and being the funny guy. Two things that I thought would bring fulfillment during that time allowed me plenty of outlets to deflect and distract myself from the anger and frustration I would feel when I would get picked on.

This worked well but quickly led to a desire to be liked by everyone regardless of what it meant I had to do or become to get that acceptance. Admittedly, it fueled me to do the very thing I hated others doing to me. Making fun of people that didn't fit in the groups I fought so hard to get in and even harder to stay in. Of course, I never did it to their face because I thought that made it better.

Fast forward to college, and full of desire to please people all the time, I joined a college fraternity and an athletic team as a cheerleader. During my freshman year, I dove headfirst into plenty of destructive behaviors around drinking and drugs to the point of selling to make extra money that my parents didn't know about.

Now about my parents, they are great people. They raised me to be well-mannered and respectful to all. Say "yes and no ma'am" and "yes and no sir." Open doors for people. Be a good person. I learned so much about work ethic, responsibility, resilience, drive, and motivation from my parents because they desired to give me all the things and more they couldn't have or didn't have the opportunity to have growing up. And they did just that. I rarely had a want I didn't get and definitely had everything I needed.

But what was produced with all of that is someone who suppressed emotions, put a smile on my face regardless of what was happening because that is the good Southern thing to do, and believed that I could get anything I wanted if I could figure out who it was going to come from. Used in the right way, it was beneficial. However, how I was using it was rather destructive. Trust me. You may be able to relate.

This is the opening scene overview of the first 18-20 years of my life. Just by reading the spark notes, anyone could see a few moments where I would have liked things to be different. Things to be easier. Things to be simpler. Things to be less hurtful. And while at the same time, I have come to realize that if any of that changed, I would not be who I am today.

Far too often, we assign our past the role of the villain and us the victim. We fall into the trap of blaming our past for who we are instead of thanking the past for who we have and are becoming. Every moment we have been given the emotional power of memory has shaped us into who we are today. To go back and change one thing would change everything.

To play out one part of my story to prove my point. If my teenage parents had stayed together, I would probably not have grown up in Louisiana. If I had not grown up in Louisiana, I wouldn't have met my first youth pastor, who had progressed to an executive pastor role in Oklahoma that gave me an internship at a church in the Tulsa, OK, area. If I didn't have the internship, I wouldn't have met the woman who is now my wife. I had not met her, I wouldn't have moved to Tulsa after college and stayed for the last eight years of my life, and ultimately, you would not be reading this now if I could go back and change one thing that for too many times in my life wished could have been different. See how that worked.

So, it is important to understand that our story matters, regardless of the pain, joy, laughter, & tears. It is the one we got written for us. Our responsibility is to accept the chapters written before today and be grateful for the lessons learned in our story as it produces who we are today.

Today, I am a husband that is incredibly happily married to an amazing woman who has broken down walls and seen the parts of me I never thought I'd show to anyone, and she loves me the same. I am a father of a daughter who amazes me daily in that I speak life, truth, and potential over every day. I am a leader who has led over two-thousand people on various leadership teams in my career. I coach and mentor them to acknowledge their story for what it is and pick the pen up as they write a future that they only see with their eyes closed. I am a coach who guides individuals and companies to evaluate current realities, present opportunities, & future projections to scale well beyond what is currently believed for.

When I stopped trying to wish my past was different, I believed the future could be as I desired, and I believe the same for you.

So how do we apply this?

1. Acknowledge where we live in the past.
2. This may be the first time you have confronted where this is true for you, and that is okay. Awareness of something is the first step to changing it.
3. Become committed to accepting that all of it, good and bad is what it is.
4. Whether that is talking about it to a friend or mentor, hiring a coach to help you through it, or, if needed, going to a professional to work through the past, we will all have to deal with it at some point, so we need to commit to the work so we can get to the fun part of the process.
5. Decide to embrace the present reality and dream for a future yet to happen.
6. Once we acknowledge where this happens and commit to processing our story, we get to take account of where we are currently and start to dream for what is to come.
7. Enjoy a future that matters.

8. What is the result of this, a future full of life and legacy? This will allow you to take others on the journey of discovery to do the process for growth.

Doing this doesn't mean we will never come face to face with things that diminish the story being written and the one we have lived. I believe it means we understand our story matters, and people are waiting for us to believe more for ourselves so they can believe the same for themselves. You can embrace the suck and success of your story and finally throw away the desire to wish your past was different because now you know it is what makes you special.

Your Story Matters!

4

FROM ESPN AND HEARTBREAK TO GOD'S PERFECT PLAN

MOLLY TROTTER GOMEZ

At the age of 14, we discover a few things about ourselves. We start learning about the opposite sex, our bodies and emotions are in full swing of development, and responsibilities start piling on. Very few at this age discover what they want to do for the rest of their lives, but at 14, it was clear that I wanted to be a storyteller. I wanted to be the person in the news when you turned on the tv, telling a new story every day. Something different, right?

Over the next eight years, I put my foot in many doors to catch my break in getting hired by a tv news station - and I did! I was beyond excited to start my career as a storyteller. I quickly realized the stories being told and how this industry was run weren't like I imagined. Living paycheck to paycheck, being put in harm's way every week, and let's not forget the emotional demands you had to deal with seeing devastating story after story. It wasn't until three years into this career that I started standing up for my voice, safety, and quality of life, while others in the industry chose to stay low and not rock the boat.

Along the way, I did find love. I met someone I had a lot in common with and wanted to spend the rest of my life with. This was someone that had not only a heart for God, which is very important to me, but also a man with a heart to serve and many ambitions in life, including serving his country. What a catch, right? I thought so. We knew this love was something different and knew this was it for us. It wasn't until he got into Army Ranger School that I realized he was someone I couldn't live without. We had the type of love that we would write to each other, and it wasn't until weeks later that we would get each other's mail sharing what was on our hearts wishing for the other person to come home at that very moment. On our first Christmas together, he asked my parents for permission to marry me with a custom-made engagement ring. I couldn't be more excited to see how he would ask me to be his wife!

Then it happened. A message from someone I didn't recognize. The type had had your head turn sideways, and your heart sinks all at the same time. A message that unloaded some of the most unbearable news that the love of my life had chosen to give himself to another woman, and she had no idea about me. When she realized what she had done, she mustered up the courage to let me know about his unfaithfulness.

So, there I was, in a job that was sucking my soul and an unfaithful relationship, wondering what I was to do next.

I remember like it was yesterday, getting a text from him saying, "I'm selling your ring back to the jewelers." I couldn't believe my eyes. Thinking, "how could someone justify saying such hurtful words?!" And at the same time, crumbling on the inside and feeling like a fool for still wanting to be with them.

I am thinking to myself, this is a crossroads many women face. Men who don't know how to express that it's over for them decide to cheat. And women wondering, "do I take him back or move on?" I asked myself the same question and even uttered it out loud to him. Only to hear, "yes... wait... no, I can't."

I felt like a damn fool. I thought, "Molly, how could you stoop so low to ask someone who clearly doesn't want you to take you back... AND THEN he says no?!"

Crushed. Devastated. Furious. But most of all, broken.

But that's not even the worst part. The most gut-wrenching part of it all was to know that my dad gave his blessing for this guy to throw me away like a piece of trash and move on to the next. That's what really broke me but fired me up (in a powerful way) at the same time.

But wait, there is more!

After nearly five years of giving my all in my news career, I was fired for a before, and after body transformation picture I posted. Yes, you heard correctly. A picture of me losing weight and inspiring others was grounds to fire me. Are you kidding me? Talk about a new low. Seriously, you couldn't go lower from here. However, oddly enough, I felt peace and a weight lifted, like these burdens were finally off of me. It's an unexplainable feeling considering I should have felt depressed after all of that.

On top of it all, I had people close to me decide it was a good time to share that I let them down by getting fired because it was "cool" to share with their friends that they knew someone on television.

The low I was at got lower at that point, and I had to decide how long I would stay down there. So, who's ready for the turning point in this story?

Looking back at it, I am unbelievably grateful I decided to get a taste of entrepreneurship before I left the news industry altogether. Network marketing was the saving grace that caught me on this fall and showed me a way out. This industry gave me the tools I needed to grow as a person, professionally and spiritually, all at the same time while being of service to others. The confidence in the company I was a part of and the mindset I developed gave me the push I needed to make a decisive move forward.

After packing up my car with everything I could fit, selling the rest, and moving to Southern California with $2,000 in my bank account and a mound of credit card debt, I was ready for my new chapter into the world of entrepreneurship.

From a friend's couch to extended family taking me in and then moving out on my own, I did whatever I could to hold to the vision of all this life experience not to be in vain. God had a purpose and plan for all of this pain!

I had moments where all the money I had was what I collected out of my car and change jar. But never once did I question God's plan for me. Even through a few heartbreaks along the way, I still trusted my time was coming.

Nearly four years later, I am married to my best friend. I am growing a sales team for a digital marketing company headed toward becoming an 8-figure company. My husband and I get to set other couples and singles free from the bondage of the lies that surround us, saying we aren't worthy or good enough to hold out for the one God has created especially for you, called the God GVN couple show every Monday night at Facebook Live.

I have seen a lot of women put up with emotional, physical, and mental abuse, thinking, "one day, he will change for me." Heck, I used to be one of them. It breaks my heart to see women and even men settling for a significant other that makes them feel less than significant because they don't want to be alone or go through the pain of starting over.

Since I have been through abusive relationships, I told myself, "it's okay to start over as many times as you need to find "your one" that God perfectly created for you. It was then that I decided, once I worked on myself and made that the focus, that a real man would see me and love me exactly how I am, flaws and all. Now that's a freeing place to be!

Now in my 30s, I've lived a lot of life where I know it's meant to be shared. Our story is meant to be mentorship to somebody else; I firmly believe that. A lot of wisdom is being kept in the dark in fear of rejection or of people not understanding. These are lies of the enemy; that enemy is Satan attacking your thoughts.

Throughout all of this, I could have given up. I could have settled for things far less than what was meant for me. Remember to ALWAYS trust the process. You only become impatient when you rush your process before you're ready. Choose to find opportunities to grow and chase your purpose. And NEVER settle.

5

FROM THE BOOK: BREAKTHROUGH

PRESTON DUCATI

"Everyone is broken by life, but afterwards some people are stronger in the broken pieces."
-Ernest Hemingway

On Christmas Eve, 1977, when I was five years old, my siblings and I had chickenpox. Although it was generally a typical illness for children, something went wrong with me. I had a terrible headache all day and night, around midnight my brother woke up from the awful noises I was making. He yelled at me to quiet down, threatening to come over to my bed and punch me. After several more warnings, he finally got up and marched over to me to deliver on his promise; he noticed something was off with me. Not only was I making weird sounds, but I was also shaking. My behavior freaked him out, and he screamed at the top of his lungs for my mom, who, seconds later, came running into our bedroom to discover that I was having a seizure. She called for an ambulance, and I was taken to the ER of a small, nearby hospital.

After a relatively quick exam, the attending doctor told my mom there was nothing they could do and that I would die. My mom let out a blood-curdling cry and collapsed to the floor (as a father of two children, I can't imagine how devastating it was for her to hear that diagnosis). A moment later, a different doctor came out and said that they were going to have an ambulance take me to Children's Hospital, believing there was a possibility that I could survive. By this time, I was in a coma.

At Children's Hospital, they began running tests on me. My mom called the pastor of our church, and he came to the hospital and prayed with her. Finally, the doctors diagnosed me with encephalitis (inflammation of the brain), an uncommon yet potentially deadly symptom of chickenpox.

As luck would have it, a pediatric surgeon named Dr. James was visiting San Diego from England at the time, lecturing about a new procedure to treat brain inflammation, the very problem threatening my life. Someone at the hospital was able to get Dr. James to come in and perform this procedure on me. It involved drilling a hole in my skull to relieve the pressure, placing a metal "screw" in the opening, and then attaching tubes to it. I remained comatose. My mom stayed at my bedside the entire time, praying for me to get better and talking to me, believing that, somehow, even in a coma, I could hear her voice and want to wake up.

Meanwhile, back at home, my grandfather, who lived in the house next to ours, planted a tree in his yard. It was a Christmas gift from my mom, and he planted it even though a powerful storm was hitting San Diego at that time. My grandpa named the tree Preston and said, "If this tree survives this storm, then so will the boy."

After over 24 hours in a coma, the storm ended. The tree survived, and so did I. The procedure had worked, and I was out of the coma. I stayed at the hospital for another five days of observation. For the next few months, they conducted weekly tests on me. But I had survived.

Still, I was mentally and physically slow for the next several years. School was not easy for me. Focusing was difficult, making reading comprehension, writing, and math difficult. Believing it was a result of everything I'd been through, my mom did not push me to do better in school. As I got older, I knew I had no choice but to work hard to overcome these obstacles.

The tree is still alive and well, and when I visit San Diego, I drive by Grandpa's old house to see it. It acts as a reminder that two of the most essential things in life are time and timing. Not only is time valuable, but we also need to appreciate the importance of timing, for example, the moments when certain people step into or out of our lives or the circumstances in our lives change.

I also learned from this experience that it's important never to allow a loss to prevent you from moving forward. This one experience at a young age could have been extremely harmful to my future. I look at it however, as a positive moment, one that I am thankful for. That moment has shaped the rest of my life and continues to be a reason why whenever I get knocked down (and I do get knocked down), I get right back up with renewed vigor. That is why I don't settle for mediocrity or allow myself to give up on any worthwhile endeavor. It's why I earned my Black Belt but continue working at advancing in the Martial Arts. It's why I keep a consistent workout regimen that continually challenges me and why I own businesses, take on challenges, invent products, and pursue my passions. It's also a big reason why I wrote this book.

We all have stories of negative experiences, no matter who you are or where you came from. We are all faced with adversity at one time or another. The goal is not to let it negatively affect you for too long. It would help if you learned to embrace and acknowledge adversity and move on as quickly as possible while embracing the right lessons from it. The goal is not to let circumstances—whether you have control over them or not—break you and make you want to give up. Don't let your story be your crutch, the reason or excuse why you can't do something. Let it be the reason why you can! What's your story, and how will it serve you to be a positive influence on your life?

We all have struggles, set-backs, and weaknesses, but you are stronger than anything that can get in your way. On the flip side, we all have successes, strengths, and triumphs. No persons story is any more valuable or important than anyone else's. Our personal story helps us develop who we are, our character, beliefs, fears, doubts, confidence, and self-esteem. We learn valuable lessons that inspire, fuel, and help us get back up when we're knocked down, even when it may seem impossible.

Our experiences create our purpose. Growing up watching David Carradine and the movies of Kung Fu Theatre on television inspired me with Martial Arts. The Chuck Norris movies like "Good Guys Wear Black," "An Eye For An Eye," and "Lone Wolf McQuade" also inspired me to set the goal of becoming a Black Belt. This was before I even knew the meaning of the word "goals." I had no sense of what it took to achieve this goal or where it might take me. I had no appreciation of how hard my brain and body would have to work, the years of commitment it would take, and how much focus, perseverance, and grit I'd have to muster to reach this objective. I just knew I needed to do it! Something make-believe had motivated me to push my body and brain further than I ever had since my brain surgery.

I started training in martial arts when I was eight years old, but it didn't last very long since my parents couldn't afford the lessons. It wasn't until I was 17 and working that I could afford classes again.

High school was tough for me, and I came close to not graduating due to bad grades and poor performance in reading and math. However, through my training in the martial arts, identifying, developing, and applying the principles that I have laid out in this book, I learned that I could far exceed my expectations and accomplish things I never thought possible during and especially after I was out of school.

Life throws negative situations and obstacles at us, and it's important to remember that these obstacles are there to help us. We don't always understand or see their purpose at the time, but they are there to create a new path and opportunity for us, and we must accept the changes they will bring.

A few years into my training, after earning my green belt (an intermediate level), I stopped training due to "unavoidable" circumstances in my life. About a month or so later I got a call from my sensei, he asked how I was and if I was ready to get back into the dojo. I realized that my situation was still ongoing and that stopping my training did not stop my "unavoidable" circumstance. So, I got my butt back in the dojo. A valuable lesson I learned about letting circumstances get in the way of achieving my goals. To this day, I'm thankful he made that call. There are many stories like this in my life, as there probably are in yours. There are people in your life that helped you get back on track. Maybe it was just a nudge, or perhaps it was a big push. Be thankful you have these people in your life. Just make sure you tell them from time to time how grateful you are for them being in your life.

This is a book about the principles and philosophies that I've acquired through many years of successes and failures. This book is about screwing up, failing, and getting back up. This is a book about grit and not giving up. It's about learning to pick yourself up off the mat and live a life that does not beat you down.

This is over thirty years of martial arts practice on paper, covering philosophies and principles about physical, mental, and emotional well-being, awareness, self-preservation techniques, and daily disciplines. It's about building a healthy relationship with yourself so that you can have a more beneficial relationship with anything or anyone. Let it help you break through circumstances and not give up when you are after something you truly desire. Most importantly, this book gives you the tools to experience a healthy, complete, and well-balanced life you love.

Live your life with purpose and never settle for just getting by. Show up as the best "you" for your community, family, friends, and life. Know your story and be thankful for it, whether joyous or painful. Life lessons are everywhere, especially underneath the negative bad experiences. It's through our reactions to those negative experiences that we either rise above or don't.

Remember: Your weaknesses can become your strengths! Your spirit is your root, grounding, and overall internal makeup. A strong spirit keeps your mind and body strong. By learning to turn our weaknesses into our strengths, our spiritual roots grow stronger.

My upcoming book will cover the importance of proper breathing, exercise, relationship building, and challenging your mind, body, and emotions. We will also dive into the mental and physical elements of awareness and personal safety.

"If you don't know yourself, you lose 100% of the time." —Ancient Samurai Proverb

The goal is to continuously work on your strengths while doing the work of turning your weaknesses into strengths. Review your strengths and weaknesses, belief systems, and overall physical, mental, emotional, and spiritual health. Live in a mindset of continuous improvement, taking small steps over time. First and foremost, when taking stock of where you stand, be honest with yourself. Lying to yourself does you no good.

What's your story?

Make a list of your weaknesses.

Make a list of your strengths.

What are some of the ideas from this chapter that you can apply to your personal life?

What ideas from this chapter can you apply to your professional life?

6

RUN OVER BY A CAR!

CHARLES CHAVEZ

"Let food be thy medicine and medicine be thy food."
-Hypocrites

I was introduced to fitness at a very young age after a very traumatic event. This event was the best and worst thing that ever happened to me. It was a paradigm shift that moved me into the health and fitness arena and changed my life forever.

At the age of 16, I was run over by a car. The year was 1978. I was a senior in high school. One month before I was to graduate, is when my life changed forever. Everyone has that one moment in time, that one monumental event in their life that changes everything and sends them into a whole new direction forever. This event was mine.

When I was initially struck by the vehicle, I flew about 15 feet in the air and landed flat on my back, hitting the back of my head hard! It was late, deep into the night, and pitch-black outside. I lay there on my back, stunned... seemingly forever. I could not tell if the stars I saw were those of the epically beautiful New Mexico sky or from the banging of my head on the cold blacktop. Time seemed to stand still, and for a brief moment, I remember being at peace. "Am I dying?" I remember thinking. I was not really scared, which seemed odd considering what had just happened. I was unusually calm and relaxed. I just laid there looking at the starry night. I remember hearing a voice coming from somewhere inside my head telling me; you're going to be alright, it's not your time, I felt at peace like I was in a surreal dream. I felt strangely comforted.

The next thing that happened I can remember like it was yesterday. A loud sound of a rumbling motor startled me out of my dream-like state, and I was suddenly wide awake and alert, then fear took over. I gasped as my lungs took in a deep breath. My eyes were wide open, my heart raced, and thundered loudly in my chest as I looked up and saw that the car was coming straight at me! Apparently, they did not hit the brake after they initially hit me. In fact, it looks like they were hitting the gas instead! I tried to call out and lift my arms to wave at them in hopes they would see me lying in the road, but I could tell they were not going to stop. Later in court, they would claim they did not see me.

I watched in horror as the headlights got bigger and bigger, coming straight at me like that possessed car Steven King wrote about in his novel Christine. The sound of the angry engine roared louder as it got closer and closer, then... PAIN! The car ran straight over me. The pain hit me so hard that it took my breath away. All I could do was grab onto anything my hands could find. They found the headers.

The car was a 1970 dodge dart, and back then, it was way cool to put headers on its powerful 350 cubic inch engine to make it sound more menacing. I still, to this day, do not have fingerprints on most of my fingers as the flesh from my hand melted on the 1000-degree pipes. I remember screaming at the top of my lungs, "stop, please stop, oh God, please stop!" over and over again. I screamed this mantra. I was so terrified. The pain of being stuck under a moving vehicle and dragged seemingly forever on the unforgiving pavement was unbearable.

The whole event must have been over in a few minutes, but as one minute may seem like no time at all to most of us, when your hand is in a flame for even a few seconds, you will find out how excruciating long one minute actually is. I felt like I was being burned alive with no hope for it ever ending. I kept screaming in hopes that someone would hear me, but the car kept going faster and faster. The pain intensified as the flesh on my body literally grated to the bone. I felt myself starting to lose consciousness. Darkness mercifully fell over me.

When the EMPs found me, my body was stuck somewhere between the blacktop of the road and the car's oil pan. Later the investigators reported that the blood streaks on the road were measured at over 650 feet. They discovered that my belt buckle had gotten lodged up onto the oil pan guard strapping me to the undercarriage of the car. Thank God that happened, or the vehicle, instead of dragging me like a tumbleweed down that dark road that night, would have steamrolled over me, crushing every bone in my body.

The ambulance ride to the hospital was excruciatingly painful. I could feel every bump on the road, and it seemed like an eternity to get to the hospital. Once there, I found myself on a table under bright lights, with doctors and nurses seemingly all around me. I heard the nurse's gasps after scissoring off my bloodied and torn clothes. I knew then it was really bad, and it was lights out again for me. When I woke the next day, I found myself in the burn ward fighting for my life.

I was seriously injured and was fighting for my life. I can barely remember the first few days in the ICU as I was so heavily medicated. I do remember pain beyond explanation or measure. Drugged up and laying in a hospital bed with legs and arms suspended in the air so the sheets would not heal onto my badly road-rashed and burned skin as I slept. I could smell my own flesh as it rotted on my body. I remember a couple of friends coming to visit and losing their cookies. Not something you want to experience when friends and family come to visit.

I spent days upon days and hours upon hours contemplating life and, more importantly, what I wanted out of life if given a chance. Reading your last rights and then told that you may never walk normally again puts a whole new perspective on what is truly important to you.

The protocols for burn patients are as bad as any torcher you could imagine. My new daily activity was being naked in a tub and scrubbed from head to toe with brushes meant to remove the dirt, asphalt, and rocks that had embedded into my torn flesh. It was a living hell, and I did not know if I would live or die. During these brutal scrubbing sessions, if given the chance, I would have chosen the latter.

I was physically and mentally exhausted, and as I lay in that hospital bed, I contemplated my life and wondered how in the hell I went from an athletic "A" student to this low point in my life. If it had not been for the love and support of my family, I don't think I would have made it. I kept thinking about that fateful night and that voice in my head telling me. You're going to be all right, and It's not your time. I don't remember the exact moment, but I decided to take full responsibility for this. To own this. To stop feeling sorry for myself and to take charge. That decision changed my life forever. You see, the whole accident really was my fault. I was hanging around with a bad crew in high school, and we liked to get into trouble. We were smoking pot, ditching classes, and drinking the day away with cheap mad dog 2020 wine. We were just kids and not bad humans. We were just all angry young boys.

The accident happened on a Friday night around 2 am. Nothing good ever happens at 2 am. What started this whole thing was a fight between one of the boys I was hanging out with and another young man from school. The fight was over a girl, of course. After school, we all got together to get high, and in our infinite wisdom, we decided to find this kid and beat the shit out of him! Well, we did end up finding him that night, and a fight did, in fact, ensue. What we did not know at the time was that he was waiting for us and had a gun. A bunch of shouting, a few punches were thrown, and a couple of gunshots later, we found ourselves in a high-speed car chase. But we were the ones being chased now! The car chase ended badly, with me stuck on the undercarriage of a car.

After my release from the hospital, I went directly into rehab. My rehabilitation involved painful physical therapy sessions to build my badly atrophied muscles up to walk properly again. I remember being bathed by my father and being waited on hand and foot by my sisters and mother. I started my rehab at a whopping 111 pounds. I had withered away to skin and bones, it seemed. But something amazing began to happen to me at the rehab center. Just a few weeks into my rehab, I noticed muscles forming on my body that I had never seen before. After about six months, I was tipping the scale at 145 pounds, and I liked it! A year later, I joined a local gym after a full recovery. I began to surround myself with humans into fitness and healthy lifestyles. I just knew in my heart that I had found my dharma!

Fast forward 30 years...

Today we as humans have so many options for fitness. We have a vast array of diet plans, fitness crazes, and new exotic therapies we can choose from. There are new terms out there like biohacking, grounding, intermittent fasting, hormesis, cryotherapy, meditation, high-intensity interval training (HIIT), plyometric training, flexibility training, boot camps, circuit, Tabata, cross fit, Pilates, myofascial foam rolling classes, and there seems to be a yoga studio or fitness center on every corner. When it comes to diets, there are so many different kinds out there that it will make your head spin. Everything from Vegan, Vegetarian, Pescatarian, Carnivore, Paleo, Keto, Fruitarian, OMAD, Zone, and Breatharians (yes, this is a real thing), just to name a few. If you are looking for alternative health hacks, you have everything from: IV Drip Therapy, Hyperbaric Oxygen Therapy, Photo Biomodulation Therapy, Compression Therapy, Infrared Sauna Therapy, NAD+Therapy, Cryogenic Chambers, Sensory Deprivation Chambers, Hugging Wellness Centers, and more.

This list goes on and on. Where does one start? When I began my personal fitness journey, it was simple. There were aerobics, strength, and endurance exercises. My diet choices were to cut carbs and cut calories. The only therapy we had back then was massage, steam rooms, dry saunas, and lots of alcohol. That's it!

To make fitness even more overwhelming these days, you have a plethora of workout facilities to choose from.

I live in Seattle, Washington, and we have hundreds of fitness studios in the Puget sound. There are dozens of yoga, pilates, indoor cycling, kickboxing, martial arts, and total body group fitness studios like Orangetheory. Some of these fitness centers have very young trainers straight out of high school that have just read an employee's manual the studio gave them and received a certificate as a bonified Master Trainer!

Where does one start if you are looking to look and feel good and get professional health and fitness guidance as well? Who can you trust to point you in the right direction? It can be overwhelming, daunting, and intimidating.

After decades of working out, thousands of hours of research, countless workshops, podcasts, and fitness events. I have practically done it all. And more importantly, I made all the mistakes for you! I have also figured out what works and what doesn't.

Our most significant discovery is that your best medicine is in nature, and the best doctor is yourself. We decided to put together an easy-to-follow step-by-step program for the everyday human. One that is more than just working out and eating a salad. There is a new science in the fitness industry called Biohacking. It involves changing the environment around you and inside of you to upgrade your body, brain, and lifespan. Biohacking consists of making small incremental diet or lifestyle changes through new technologies and ancestral living. It is growing in popularity but can be a bit confusing on where to start. So, if you are tired of being tired and ready to take back control of your life, let us help you. Check out our new book, The LifeSpanners fitness Cookbook. Your recipe to a Long, Healthy & Radically Happy Life.

7

YOUR LEGACY

SAM JOHN

"You have to know the past to understand the present."
-Carl Sagan

My parents, C.O. John and Mary John were married and are from Kerala, India. They moved from Mumbai, India, for work, got married, and got offers to move to Dammam, Saudi Arabia. My dad was an accountant, and my mom was a nurse. They were happy financially and visited medical specialists in India and Saudi Arabia. They received news that she would never become parents. During this time, they planted an underground church in their apartment in Saudi Arabia.

Many people came to our home, aka church. They fasted, prayed, and knocked on heaven's doors continually. After seven years of praying, they miraculously had me. They named me Sam for Samuel in the Old Testament, as Hannah prayed for a child in the Bible. Sure, it sounds powerful. I wasn't that impressed. Growing up as a Preacher's Kid, I was lost in my childhood to certain illegal habits (wow, that word sounds so cool).

I wasted my early teenage years. By God's divine grace, I got saved at a Christian camp. I went to that camp thinking of meeting girls! However, I experienced God personally and realized I needed Christ to change me radically. This included my mind, heart, and soul. This included cleaning up my mind of garbage, my mouth with slander, and my heart with lust, murder, and pride. Did I change overnight? No, slowly but gradually, God transformed me. He is still working in me.

Was I thankful for my past experiences? Well, No. Am I thankful today? Yes, because it helps me relate to young people and kids as they struggle through some of the same strongholds. It allows me to put an arm around their shoulder, walk with them, pray with them, joke around with them, and let them know that I was like them too. It reminds me to be humble before God and hits me hard when I almost touch the line of legalism! I also let them know that they will fall again and again, but as long as we introspectively let God (The Holy Spirit) convict us and encourages us to be like King David before God, He will start to work in us.

Your Legacy = Your Not So Impressive Past + GOD.

Over the years in school, college and university, I became active in Christian ministry through my Praise and Worship band, Faith Warriors. We went to Christian events and played at different venues, and then in early 2002, a couple of us crazy guys formed a Christian Metal band in Bangalore, India. Yes, Christian metal in India. We called ourselves Whitenoiz. Our sole intention was to reach the kids with the gospel message. We toured India extensively, having played on some of the biggest stages in India.

I thought I had arrived. In my late teens and early 20s, I saw fame, 5-star hotels, and even 15,000 people swaying to your music. This seemed to be my life purpose. That was it. I will be the world's best metal vocalist, and someday I will have a million followers on myspace, Orkut, and Facebook. Did that happen? Heck no, my band dissolved in 2010. We kept revving the engine for a couple of years with different band members, and we all moved to the Middle East, the US, Australia, and Canada. Did I achieve anything phenomenal there? Yes, the gospel message was preached. We initiated a movement for many kids to come up as Christian Rock and Metal musicians. In terms of recognition, we had a Metal Revolver magazine picture, an HM Magazine feature, an album, and a couple of shows, but my Wacken Open Air dreams never realized. I thought, In my mind, I had reached the end of my metal vocalist career, now to get serious and get busy with family.

I thought to myself in my years after that. Why did I go through that phase? What was the purpose behind it? Why did it end? After thinking deeply, I realized a few things.

1. I was exposed to fame and glory in my teen years, which gave me a mature outlook on the meaning of fame, the experience of glory and pain.

2. I was exposed to being onstage.

3. I could express my faith in the most authentic way possible by writing songs from my heart

I was able to impact a generation of kids who probably didn't have anyone else show the way.

That was enough! Fast forward to 2014, I arrived in Toronto, Canada, as Permanent Resident, Skilled Person category. The first time I walked the streets of downtown Toronto, I quickly realized that people in Canada need Jesus. I didn't know that the world here was post-Christian. Canada was a Christian country; at least, that's what I thought when I was in India. I went to a great church close to home, but God didn't leave me. I used to have this burden follow me for the next two and a half years.

I decided to pray with my wife, did prayer drives and walks, and after seeking the Lord in late 2017, I planted a church in Toronto called Church Underground. I just told God; I'm going to step into this call. All I want is for YOU to step in. I don't mind failing, and I don't care about failure, my ego, or people's opinion about my attempt to launch a church.

BUT GOD, please, please show up. I am not doing this for me. I am not doing this for income. Even today, I am a co-vocational Pastor. I work full-time during the week and volunteer at church. He never left my side. He is the one that poured out the passion in me. We have about 7 to 8 million people in the Greater Toronto, Hamilton Area. It is growing fast, and people don't usually attend church. We need more churches! Today my call is to develop leaders and plant gospel-believing, word-based, spirit-based churches in North America. All the people of the world are migrating and moving to North America for one reason. To hear the good news of the gospel.

While leading the church, that's when everything hit me. The experience of being an Indian origin preachers kid, a church planters kid, saved from addiction, the Christian metal call, my strong family upbringing, and my intellectual quest for the existence of God all came together as I started to teach at church. I was able to meet a couple of guys in Toronto, and we also launched a metal band here and have opened for American bands War of Ages, Oh Sleeper, Stryper and many other secular and satanic bands. The stage belongs to Him wherever we go, and The Holy Spirit moves. How was this possible for an

Indian kid raised in Bangalore, India, to even witness these bands play live and to open their show as the exclusive band? Only God knows that.

In 2020, my Indian band Whitenoiz my Indian band regrouped with our initial band lineup during COVID. We remotely studio re-recorded our first single Crush, while I was in Canada, our bass player in Australia, our guitar player, keyboard player, and drummer now in the States.

Your Legacy = Your Shattered Dreams + God

Ephesians 2:10 says, "For we are his workmanship, created in Christ Jesus for good works, which God prepared beforehand, that we should walk in them."

I want to encourage you today. I want to tell you ONLY one thing. Your history, background, upbringing, skin color, financial history, and abuse! Everything has a meaning. It seems tough to imagine. It sometimes feels painful. But Everything can be used by God. Yes, you heard me. You are made uniquely by God. You are made in the image and likeness of our Creator.

You have a UNIQUE PURPOSE. Every experience, chaotic situation, disruption, distraction, and every unfulfilled dream will turn out to be a blessing if only you LET GOD Tie it all together. He knows your end from the beginning. It's about Him and what He can do through you and your past. Your story matters! And You Matter!

If you need someone to talk to, feel free to reach out to me on Instagram or Facebook. I can pray for you.

8

FROM THE BOOK: STILL STANDING

LATOYA ANDREWS

"There is no growth without change, no change without fear or loss, and no fear or loss without pain."
-Rick Warren

When we were children, we had hopes, dreams, and big imaginations. We knew what we wanted to be, how big our house would be, and what kind of car we would have. Everything was simple and stress-free. Then we grow up, and life takes over. Somewhere between childhood and adulthood, I lost my focus. I was going through the motions while life was passing me by. I have always been a loner, even as a child.

I felt like I was different from everyone, INVISIBLE. No one cared, and no one loved me filled my thoughts. And as an adult, it didn't get any better. I was used and abused and never spoke up for myself. I allowed people to walk all over me. After I met my husband and married him, I envisioned things going completely differently. All I wanted was someone to finally show me the love and attention I was yearning for. But apparently, his definition of love and my definition were completely different.

Now a grown woman, married with children. Wow, I was clueless about everything. I didn't know the first thing about being a woman, wife, or mother. But I learned the hard way, with trial and error. My life seemed to get harder and harder. I was in a one-sided marriage; my opinion or feelings did not matter. I had low self-esteem and no confidence, felt like I was ugly, and did not like myself. Many of my decisions were only to please the man, to keep them happy. I tolerated and accepted the abuse. I was not happy with the person that I had become.

When I looked in the mirror, I did not recognize the person staring back at me. My husband wanted me to be someone that I was not comfortable with. But I did it anyway to keep him happy. Growing up, I imagined my marriage to be very different. The cheating, the lying, the heartache, the abuse, it was very hard and painful. I was with my husband for 14 years until he passed in October 2012. After my husband, I thought I had a better grip on things.

But after a while, I found myself back on that familiar path. Living my life for a man and not focusing on the right things. I didn't understand and often asked God, "Why?" "What did I do that was so bad to deserve these things happening to me?" I wasn't a bad person and was very respectful, a quiet child. People were selfish and inconsiderate, only caring about themselves and their desires. At this point, I was tired and overwhelmed. Something had to change.

More and more people are finding themselves in these types of relationships. They give up their power to the other person and basically give up on life or change the situation. My life was slowly passing by, and I was not happy. I realized something was wrong with me. I finally decided that I needed counseling for all the pain and trauma I had endured.

In doing so, I discovered that a lot of my issues and problems stemmed from suppressed feelings and memories from when I was a kid. Because I did not have anyone to talk to about it then, they were able to manifest, causing problems in my adult life. As a child, it was tough to understand how adults could do those things to me; they knew it was wrong. I felt like nobody cared about me. I didn't feel loved. My cousins and other kids would call me names, and I believed them. I was invisible to all. Talking to the counselor, I could finally get it all out. My deep soul search helped me to get everything out of my head and on paper. My life testimonies, and now I am sharing them with everyone. I am releasing my first book called, "Still Standing."

None of this would have been possible without God. After the depression, trauma, hurt, abuse, and disappointment, I allowed Him to heal me and guide me in the direction he needed me to go. I am here for His purpose. He is shaping and molding me for this reason. God allows us to experience things to make us stronger.

Every situation that life throws at us has a reason and a life lesson behind it. Once you open yourself up to God, He can change you and the situation. He wants to help us. My eyes have been opened, and my life perspective has changed. I am living proof that God CAN change it. My past is my past. I have learned from my mistakes and how to forgive. Regardless of how others treated me, I have never allowed it to change me or my heart.

Some people use this as an excuse to mistreat someone else. Because they were hurt, they are going to make you hurt. That is not right to do. I am a helper, always willing to give. And if I don't have it, I will figure out a way. I do what God puts on my heart to do. If you take advantage of me or do wrong to me, I will not seek revenge. I will just put it in God's hands and let Him deal with you. I have never been able to intentionally hurt anyone. I am here to do His work.

In my new book, "Still Standing," I share my story and testimonies with all who need it. Our testimonies will bring people to the church and could inspire them to get saved. All that we endure makes us stronger and teaches us to grow in the spirit and in the church. These painful experiences also equip us for our ministry so that we can comfort others. When others are troubled, we can give them the same comfort God gives us.

Knowing who you are and what you want from life is a beautiful feeling. It gives you purpose and meaning. Hold your head high in confidence, never letting another person tear you down again. Always be yourself and change for NO ONE.

If you or anyone you know need help or having suicidal thoughts, please don't hesitate to call 1-800-273-8255. Depression is a very serious illness, DON'T take it lightly.

9

THE ACCIDENT

JOSHUA HAYES

I think about that day often. Not because of some need for the nostalgia or because I love to live in the past. If I'm being honest, it's because my sense of wonder has grown after 16 years. Every time my mind drifts to that time, I have to convince myself that it actually happened.

Winters in Oklahoma have always been somewhat bipolar. Maybe manic is a better word. Either way, this particular day was only cold because of the wind chill. I bought myself a sheepskin leather jacket earlier that month using my leftover grant money from school. I felt a sense of pride when I put that jacket on because I was homeless just a couple of years prior and living out of my broken-down 1988 Ford Thunderbird. Now I'm driving an almost new Chevy S-10, wearing an expensive leather jacket, and attending a university. I had no family support and finally proved I didn't need it.

I don't really recall the class I got out of. I just remember wanting to go straight home and take a much-needed nap. I didn't live far, but I didn't live close enough to walk. Besides, who'd want to walk against an Oklahoma wind chill? Instead, I headed to my usual parking spot in front of Hastings Hall. A few months prior, I was a pizza delivery guy. That gave me a leg up on the quickest route home. I only lived about six or eight blocks away, so I should be home before my heater even warms up.

I ended up only getting half of that last sentence right. My heater never warmed up, but I also never made it home. This particular road didn't have a stop sign, so it allowed me to turn up the radio. My new favorite song, "Paint Me A Birmingham" by Tracy Lawrence, came on the radio. My fingers barely released the dial when I heard an explosion on the passenger side. I want to describe the sensation of the moment, but I only felt as if I was watching the experience from within the recesses of my mind. I didn't feel anything. Within a micro-second, my truck slid down the road on its driver's side. I saw the glass explode like crystal popcorn and disappear underneath my right arm, which was skiing on the exposed asphalt just inches from my face.

After what seemed like an eternity, my truck finally stopped about thirty yards from the intersection. When my mind caught up with my body, I realized I was being suspended from the ground by my seatbelt. I quickly pressed the release and dropped to the ground. Landing on the roadway that had been flirting with my face just seconds earlier. As I stood up, I noticed that the top of my head was touching the passenger window. I attempted to open the door, but it was crushed in. However, the window didn't even have a blemish on it. Without thinking, I punched straight up and shattered the glass. I then grabbed the window frame and jumped out like a monkey escaping a snake's den.

I took a moment to gather my thoughts and make sense of the scene. It looked as if my truck had lost a wrestling match with a

The Accident

bulldozer. On the crossroad was the bulldozer—a gray early 1980's Buick with a delivery driver sign on the roof. I needed to figure out what had happened, so I headed to the Buick. I took two steps and woke up in the back of an ambulance. I must've been out a few minutes because I woke up to a police officer asking me where the screwdriver was. This puzzled me completely, so I had to hear him again before I accepted it as an honest question. Still unsure of the question, I told him I didn't have one and wasn't sure why I needed one. He looked at me, almost puzzled, and said, "To break the glass. You do realize that Buick couldn't even break it?" Apparently, he had never been trapped in a vehicle before.

The next several weeks were somewhat fuzzy. When I say fuzzy, I mean I don't remember anything. Well, nothing except the pain and weakness. I ended up hiring an attorney with a massive advertisement on the back of a phonebook. His first order of business was to send me to a chiropractor. I only went a couple of times before the chiropractor, who was pretty much anti-modern medicine, said I needed an orthopedic surgeon.

The first orthopedic surgeon I saw had me do an MRI scan of my back. Basically, you get rolled into this Closter phobic tube, and it takes pictures of your innards that an x-ray can't. When we got the results, the doctor said nothing was wrong and I probably just had strained muscles. At this point, I'm walking with a cane and am in so much pain that I dropped out that semester. My attorney then sent me to a neurosurgeon who spoke English as a second language or maybe even a third language. He hooked me up to some machine that checked nerve pulses. I told him I was in extreme pain and couldn't feel my legs. He all but called me a liar. His fancy machine knew my body better than me. All while dealing with doctors and pain, my attorney went radio silent. A few weeks later, he finally called me back. He tells me he sent an offer to the delivery company. I assume he thought this was good because he acted like a border collie who brought you a dead rodent. I did the only sensible thing I could think of. I fired him!

I don't recall how I found Mark, my new attorney. I just remember my first meeting with him. He was a no-nonsense type of guy and an obvious rancher. He still had cow manure on his boots. I instantly liked him. I told Mark about my doctor troubles, and he sent me to my third and final doctor.

Dr. Mayoza was straight out of Louisiana. It was obvious from his accent. When he got my MRI scans, he found my issue pretty quickly. He showed the part of my lower back that should have discs; apparently, mine had been crushed. He then told me the solution was simple. He will put two rods in my back and create some disks from my hip. I was going to have a multi-level disc fusion. According to the doc, "this sounds worse than it is. It's a two-hour surgery followed by a few months rest. You'll be back to school in no time," he said.

About a month later, I found myself in the hospital's Pre-Op room. The nurse was about to introduce me to the anesthesiologist, but first, I had to read a waiver. I'll be honest. I wasn't that nervous up until this point. I'm not sure if it was my youthful ignorance or me urgently ready to stop walking with a cane. Thank God the anesthesiologist came next. I didn't realize the surgery alone could paralyze me or leave me defecating from a bag. The nurse reassured me that no one would have the surgery if even a small fraction ended up with one of these detriments. After that conversation, my meeting with the anesthesiologist was a complete blur, but at least his visit came with a shot that knocked me out cold.

Waking up was like being plastered drunk and hung over at the same time while trying to figure out why I don't remember fighting an eight-hundred-pound gorilla. The world was spinning, and for some reason, I couldn't brace my foot on the floor to stop it. I heard someone repeating my name, but all I wanted was a drink of water. I couldn't quite get the words out, so I kept putting my hands to my lips.

Finally, someone started feeding me ice chips. The nurse said I couldn't have anything else until the doctor arrived. It didn't matter anyway. I must've dosed off. I woke up to Dr. Mayoza saying my name. I was much more coherent this round and could see it was already night again. I thought I had to have slept all day. Dr. Mayoza had this puzzled look on his face, and I could tell he had something he wanted to say. Without hesitation, he said the four words I've been asking ever since.

"How were you walking?" Confused, I asked him to clarify. That's when he told me the surgery did not take two hours. It was an eleven-hour surgery. Dr. Mayoza said, "Mr. Hayes, open heart surgeries don't last that long." All I could do was stare at him while he explained what had happened. What he expected to find was just a pair of defective discs. What he actually found was a crushed disc, a dead disc, and a severed spinal cord at the L-4 part of my back. The spinal cord was embedded into my vertebra, and it took a while to remove it. The good news was that I had so much calcium build up from my bone spurs that he didn't have to remove bone from my hip to use as a filler in the fusion. The bad news was that he didn't know what my future held.

My spinal cord was completely severed. By all scientific reasoning, I should not have been walking. For the next half hour, I just sat and listened to Dr. Mayoza explain the possibilities of my future. However, if I'm honest, none of his words affected me. He couldn't explain my past. How in the hell was he going to dictate the potential of my future?

That first day was not very productive. Except for once every two hours, I stayed asleep. Now that second day, that was a home wrecker. I didn't take the pain meds or push that morphine button nearly as often as I probably should. I woke up to this pain that felt like my new titanium screws were literally unscrewing out of my back. The doc came in to check on me. After being scolded for not taking medicine before I started hurting, he directed my future ex-wife to push the button for me. Whatever they put in that I.V. must've been the secret formula because I was trying to convince the nurses to let me try walking. Unfortunately, in my mind, I had to wait for the doctor's permission. Given that decisive "no" answer, I spent the rest of the day watching bad television and thinking about those four words. "How were you walking?"

The following day, the nurse came in and told me that Dr. Mayoza had given me permission to start walking. I asked if I had to have help, and she just gave me a sideways laugh. I was serious. I slid my legs and feet off the bed, thankful I still had that ability and attempted to thrust myself up. It was at that moment that I completely understood the nurse's laugh. I not only needed help to walk, but I looked like I was trying to poop while rocking forward in complete chagrin. Thankfully the nurse kept her comments to herself, although I would have laughed with her. She quickly came over and helped me stand for the second first time in my life.

For that day, I never went further than the restroom, but I made sure that I got up. On one of my walks, I asked the nurse when I'd be able to leave. She said it depended on how much I walked, but it was typically one and a half weeks. She said the doctor needed to know that I would be okay without having any nurses around. With those words, I started walking more. I still needed assistance, and it never stopped hurting, but it did get easier. Three days later, I was headed home! The doctor must've put something extra with my regular pain medication. I was on cloud nine, and that two-hour trip home only lasted about five minutes.

According to Doctor Mayoza, my recovery time was expected to last two years. He said it's half that time typically, but my injury was extraordinary and required much more attention. His advice was not to push myself and to take my pain medication before I started hurting. The first half, I didn't listen to. The second half, I shouldn't have listened to. For the first couple of months, all I did was rest. However, I started getting cabin fever and the idea of two years of this was out of the question. As soon as I could walk with a walker, I started stretching. I would pour a couple of cups of Epsom salt into a bath of slightly less than scolding hot water. I would soak in this for about half an hour. I would immediately have my future ex-wife help me stretch until it hurt.

After about four months, I could walk without assistance. I never could find the answer to those four words, but I wasn't going to let that miracle go to waste. I wasn't going to be a desk jockey. I wasn't going to be forced to do anything. I was only 24. I needed options.

Within a few months, I left a message with Dr. Mayoza asking if I could start training in Tae Kwon Do. I got a pretty quick response of "no." I then called back. I explained that I did not want to compete in contact sports, but the art itself helps tune your agility and fitness. He finally agreed on the condition that I did not fight. I believe that decision alone propelled my recovery to the next level. It wasn't very long before I felt no one could tell I was disabled at all. I hated calling myself disabled, but I knew that's how the world saw me.

I started going to the psychology club meetings with my future ex-wife. They needed a guest speaker. I asked my friend, that's a narcotics officer, to speak. After the meeting, I asked him if you were disqualified from being a police officer if you had any back surgeries. He told me that disabilities are a protected class and that if I can pass the agility, they can't deny me. It was at that moment that I got excited about my future. In no time, I was working at the county jail and making plans to become a police officer. I'd like to say that I got hired on my first test. However, I failed miserably at the mile-and-a-half run. When has a cop ever had to run a mile and a half before? After about five months of working as a detention officer, I finally got another chance. This time, I wouldn't fail.

For eleven years, I served as a police officer. I continued working out and going to the gym. I stayed in better shape than many of my counterparts. At one point during my recovery, I was tempted to get on disability. The doctors labeled me as one hundred percent disabled without the possibility of recovery. However, those four words kept repeating in my head. "How were you walking?" It was those words that told me not to quit.

The voice inside my heart said that no one puts limits on me without my permission. I walked because neither I nor God gave my body permission not to. We have only two choices in life, we either do, or we don't. It is always up to us. Listen to your body. Listen to your heart, and listen to your soul. Remember, several doctors said nothing was wrong. My body did. I was told not to push myself, but my heart said to do it. Finally, no one said I could become a cop, but my soul said no one could stop me.

10

THE ROSE THAT GREW FROM CONCRETE

BROOKE KELLY

The glass shattered into a million little pieces as I stumbled through the glass door in pain. My mind couldn't help but blame myself for what was happening. "It's my fault the door is broken, and it's my fault she had to throw me through it." As I stood up and looked at her, the physical pain I was enduring was no comparison to the mental and emotional pain running through my mind. "I get treated like this because of who I am and the things I do. I deserve this because I'm bad, and no one will ever want to love me because of who I am." My head dropped to my chest, eyes to the ground as she verified my thoughts with her words. This is just one incident that I encountered at the age of seven that would have a long-term impact on the person I would one day become and who I am still growing into being.

Today, as I read through the letters handed over to the court system in an attempt to remove me from this nightmare, I am reminded of so many memories my brain had trained itself to forget. There were reports from neighbors of screams and sounds of panic and fear coming from my living hell. Gossip of abuse painted my small town, but no one understood what I was going through.

When they would see me, I seemed unsettled, insecure, withdrawn, and quiet. It was rare to catch me smiling, and I could not make eye contact with adults. I looked malnourished and was usually ill due to lack of care. I behaved poorly in school on purpose. My only goal in school was to receive attention; the easiest way to do that was negative attention. My father placed me on medications for ADHD, ADD, and depression instead of getting to the true root of the problem. Can you believe that? I was medicated for depression at the age of 8, and my father happily fed me the pills in an attempt to no longer inconvenience his own life.

But this is only part of the story. Aside from all the physical torment I was dealing with at that time, I lacked many of the critical elements needed to raise and develop a mentally and emotionally strong female child. This was only heightened when my father decided he didn't want me anymore and signed his rights over to my grandmother. Which I later would find out as an adult would give me "abandonment issues" that I would have to overcome with little support. In addition to the fact that my father chose to place me in the care of someone who beat me while neglecting my most basic needs, I also lacked the care and love from my mother.

You see, it was a disease. That's what she would tell us anyway. I rarely got to see her, and when I did, it was only for short periods due to her inability to remain coherent. I will never forget the morning I woke up for school and just so happened to walk into the living room when the news was on. I remember listening to the news anchor telling the story of two young boys found in diapers walking down Sheridan Road in the middle of the day. Luckily, a stranger found them walking and called the police.

The news anchor finishes the story, showing the woman responsible for the wandering children. There she was, my mother, on the local news. She had been passed out drunk on the couch, and my two little brothers had left the apartment alone. They ended up walking down a seriously dangerous street with no shoes or clothes at only two and three years old. After losing custody of her three children because of substance abuse, this "disease," as she called it, allowed her to lose my youngest two brothers to the system. Five kids. She had five kids and was unable to provide for, love, or nurture any of us.

As I got older, I didn't realize the aftermath effects my childhood would have on my adult life. Mentally, emotionally, spiritually, and relationally. I had to retrain my brain to what was "healthy" and "unhealthy." I ended up in unhealthy relationships with men who didn't love or respect me, used and abused me in the same ways I was treated as a child. This is what love is, right? Being controlled was just his way of showing that he loved and cared about me.

Those are the types of things I thought were normal. Although I put myself in those situations and had to learn the hard way, God used each one of those relationships to reveal to me a different area of my life that I had an unhealthy mindset. Each relationship served a specific purpose, and it was my place to either learn from the relationship or continue living in unhealthy cycles. This was hard for me! Since I had abandonment issues, it was hard for me to let people go. I would forgive the most unforgivable things and continue to subject myself to unloving behavior over and over. I like to think that this is something I have finally grasped, but it took many years of pain, prayers, and counseling sessions to get me to where I am now. I would be lying if I told you that this is something that I have mastered and that I have all the answers. This is something that I will struggle with for the rest of my life, but I am at least aware of my thoughts and reactions to things, which I can redirect into healthy ones. Ultimately, it is up to me whether I choose to control and understand these struggles the best I can or if I let them control me, and the same goes for you.

These stories and my life experiences are in no way meant to depress or draw any sympathy from the readers. In fact, it is meant to do the exact opposite. God uses each of us to be a light in someone else's life, and it is our job to figure out what that light is and shine it as brightly as we can! This is part of the journey of finding our purpose.

I am currently writing my first book, "The Rose That Grew From Concrete." The goal of this book is to be completely transparent to help others relate and see that things really aren't as bad as they seem. I hope to inspire and motivate those who have been in similar life circumstances, those who need that extra push of encouragement for their next breakthrough, and those who have difficulty believing in themselves. This story, my story, was part of God's plan, and I would be failing Him and you if I didn't have the courage to share it. I believe this is part of my purpose, so I am willing to share with everyone that I can to help change someone else's life.

Throughout my book, I will explain several tools we can use that will allow us to use our past to drive us toward our passion and purpose instead of letting it bring us down and negatively define our lives. The choice is up to you! In my book, "The Rose That Grew From Concrete," I will discuss having the right mindset and how this can be a critical element in overcoming obstacles in life. Positive thinking! It seems so simple, but you would be surprised how much you can struggle with this.

There are some minor changes you can quickly make in your life to help yourself start having more of a positive, "glass is half full" type mindset.

Unfortunately, part of the aftermath of growing up without unconditional love from my parents was the inability to understand my identity. This was probably the biggest struggle I had to overcome, and many people struggle with this exact same thing. Some women are going through life without a mother or father that deal with similar issues. A few problems you might face when you don't know your identity is understanding your worth, what real love looks like, and knowing who you are in Christ. Not knowing what real love looks like was hard for me since my father never showed me what it was. He was the first man I ever loved, and he didn't even want to hold my hand at the grocery store as a child. So really understanding and knowing what love is was something I had to learn on my own.

Different struggles that come with a loss of identity don't come as easy to those of us that have been dealt a bad hand of cards in life. The importance of understanding identity isn't just for women. This section of the book is also for men. This is for anyone that might lack self-confidence, doesn't understand their purpose or people that connects their identity to things that don't belong, being a part of who they are. Identity is huge and finding it is a game changer. I hope to play a small role in helping you find your authentic self.

Many of the personal struggles we deal with point right back to self-awareness. For me, I am extremely hardheaded. Twenty different people could tell me what and how to do something or how to handle a situation, but more than likely, I will probably do it the way I want to anyway.

Well, that was before I understood what self-awareness was. Once I can recognize this about myself, I can make a cognitive effort to rationalize counsel from other people before blowing it off completely. Knowing what areas of our lives we are weak in and need to improve is the first step. Then taking the necessary measures to improve in those areas is vital. Once you can understand the principles used to become self-aware and then consciously apply them to yourself, you are literally unstoppable.

I'm sure you've heard the saying, "you are your biggest competition." This is exactly what that saying means: recognize areas of weakness, the barriers, and how to overcome them. Being self-aware is a strength that will help move you toward your purpose, and I want to help you dig deep and find out how to do that.

What jumpstarted this whole thing, you are probably asking? What happened in my life that made me wake up one day and start to think about my plan and then put my plan into action? I was in a horrible relationship in 2016, which encouraged me to start attending church. As I began my genuine journey with Christ, this set the whole mood for me.

Here I am. When I tell you I am far from perfect, I mean that. I don't have all the answers and have made many mistakes in my life. But because of God's grace, I can say that I am proud of myself for who I am and who I am becoming. When I could slowly start applying some of these principles to my life, I started seeing growth in all areas of my life. It took a lot of maturing, a lot of self-analyzing, and me just being sick and tired of being in situations I was putting myself into.

In 2017 I received my Real Estate license and was named top 13th Tulsa realtor on social media in 2018. Towards the end of 2017, I began working on my master's degree and graduated in December 2019. Looking over at the crowd as I walked across that stage, I was reminded of what I had overcome to get to this point. Not only did I graduate, but I completed the Master of Business Administration program with honors. Having accomplished these things are great, but what was more meaningful to me is what I went through to get there.

I knew if I could do this, the girl that was told she would never be anybody by her own father, that she would live in Section 8 housing her whole life, then anybody could. I knew I wanted to be a voice for other people that are having a hard time overcoming their pasts but are trying to move forward. That is when I decided I wanted to write a book. I want other people to understand that they don't have to allow what they have been through define who they are.

Ultimately the choice is up to you what you will and won't allow to flow through your life. I hope this book speaks to you in more ways than one and helps push you to the next level. There is hope and a light at the end of the tunnel.

Stay on the lookout for more of my story in my upcoming book, "The Rose That Grew From Concrete," where I will dive much deeper into my story. My story is about beauty, self-preservation, growth, modalities, and breakthroughs.

11

THE DAY I BURNED MY HOUSE DOWN

GARY LUNSFORD

I was seventeen years old in 1980 on that cold December afternoon when I was given the task of cutting wood for the night's heat in an old farmhouse that my parents had rented on a hillside in a country setting a few miles from Mercerville, Ohio when it happened. I had carried into the living room of that old farmhouse the wood I had just cut and placed some onto the fireplace grate. It was the only heat source except when the stove was turned on in the kitchen to help warm things up.

There were nine of us living there at the time of the fire, but not everyone was there that evening. My parents were in town at the company Christmas party to get my Dad's Christmas bonus which we needed badly with all of us kids, one sister was at a basketball game at the High School playing in the band, and three of the littlest ones were at our Grandparents house for the night which left three of us boys, myself being the oldest left at home. Me and one brother were standing in front of the fireplace while the other brother was lying on the couch watching the color TV we had just gotten, and that's when it happened.

I couldn't get the wood to catch fire. I had put it in the grate because it was green, so I decided to pour gasoline on it from the gallon for the chainsaw I had used to cut the wood with. So, I poured some on there, then lit it, and WOOOSH, it caught fire and quickly burned off most of the gasoline except for a few flames. Then I decided to take the jug before the rest of the flames went out and throw some more on it, but when I did, it combusted, huge flames!

I pulled the milk jug with the gasoline back towards me and held it in my hand. I looked and saw flames on the top by the mouth and thought if this hits the remaining gasoline, it will catch the whole thing on fire and explode and catch my brother standing beside me on fire and me. Thinking I only had a few seconds before it happened, I turned and threw it in the kitchen, and when it hit the floor, it spread!

I quickly grabbed a blanket and tried to put it out but to no avail. As I hit the fire, hoping to put it out, it also caught the blanket on fire! That old farmhouse that sat on that hillside caught fire; since it was two stories, it spread to the kitchen ceiling and took off from there. Thankfully my brothers and I all got out safely! But then I saw our cat needed to get out of the house, so I ran through the side door, grabbed the cat, and went out another door on the other side. Now I'm on one side of the house, and my brothers are on the opposite side.

As a seventeen-year-old immature kid afraid of getting in trouble, I ran into the woods. I went along the ridge until I got as far away from the house as possible. Some people started showing up, so I crossed the highway and went to the other side, went up into the woods on the opposite hillside, and watched that old farmhouse burn! With all our material possessions, including Christmas presents, all of it, burn to the ground!

It was winter, it was cold, and I was scared! There were gas tanks behind the house hooked up to the kitchen stove, but when the fire got near them, thankfully, they didn't explode. However, the gas inside caught fire at the nozzle and shot a flame out 4 to 6 feet long and was so loud, releasing the flaming gas that it sounded like a loud airplane engine going down a runway. I watched as people came from different places to help, but there was nothing they could do. It burned to the ground that cold December night in 1980.

So, what would any rational teenager do in this situation? I decided to run away! No way was I going to face the consequences of what happened, so I went down the hillside, got to the highway, and headed toward Mercerville. Not far down the road, a kid from school I knew stopped his vehicle and picked me up for a ride. He said, "hey Gary, what are you doing?" And I answered, "I just burnt my house down." He replied, "you did not burn your house down!" Not believing what I had just told him, some Emergency vehicles passed us heading toward the house!

I just wanted to go as far as possible in the opposite direction! When he saw those vehicles, He said, "You did burn your house down!" Then he wanted to turn around and take me back there, and I told him, "no, I'm running away!" He was finally able to talk me out of it, so I let him drop me off at my grandparent's house, where my father was.

As you can imagine, I did not want to see my father's face. I mustered up all the courage I could and walked inside. There was my dad, and to my surprise, he did not get angry with me. He was just glad that we survived! We lost all our stuff in that fire, but all nine of us were alive and well. Our Grandparents let us stay there until we found another house. I couldn't believe it.

People kept stopping by to help us, giving us all sorts of things to help us get back on our feet.

We returned to the house the next day or a few days later and looked at our home in ruins. It was burnt to the ground except for the stones that the front porch sat on. There were ashes everywhere! As I looked around, nothing was left that I remember until I found a ceramic-shaped Bible that we had. It was the only thing I found that survived our house fire in December 1980. That was a "sign" to me! It was a point in time that God used to show me no matter how bad that fire got in all its destruction, that His Word WILL survive it!

But Gary, it was just a ceramic Bible. It wasn't a real bible some might say. I know, but it represented His Word, and let me tell you personally that I did not go to that house looking for a sign from God. I was not that type of person. But God was looking to get my attention through this. Let me tell you that it was not just a coincidence because I have personally heard stories from other fires that burned other houses throughout my life, yet out of the ruins, The Bible had survived them, not being burned up. There are too many of them to prove otherwise.

I believe that God is saying to us that "No matter how the fire started," "No matter how hot the fire got," "No matter how much the fire has destroyed," "No matter how many ashes it has left in your life," My WORD which is My Son, Jesus Christ, has walked through your fire and is there waiting for you to find Him. He is the "Sign" that you are really looking for as you search through the ashes for something of value.

He is there in your ashes as "Precious" for you to take hold of. God placed Him there to find you, for you are "Precious" to Him. Jesus, with His hand out, is saying to you, "I will give you beauty for ashes." For My Father, God has said...

Isaiah 61:3 (KJV) says, "To appoint unto them that mourn in Zion, to give unto them beauty for ashes, the oil of joy for mourning, the garment of praise for the spirit of heaviness; that they might be called trees of righteousness, the planting of the LORD, that he might be glorified."

Take Me "The Word of God" by believing in me. (Read John 3:16) Receive me by calling my name. (Romans 10:9-13)

I Will Give You BEAUTY for ASHES!

I grabbed ahold of Jesus after sitting in the ashes, and He has proved to me that He is precious, and I am precious to him. He has given me beauty for ashes! He is the real deal, the real answer to real-life problems. I have tasted and seen that He is good throughout the years, from that seventeen-year-old kid to an older man in The Lord. He has called me to preach His Glorious Good News through various ways to reach the people He wants to save, and one way is by writing books.

I never thought for 50-plus years on planet Earth that I would ever write a book. I didn't even want to, to be honest. But one day, I felt like the Lord wanted me to take a message He gave me and write it in a book. I did not know how to do it, so I asked Him to help me. Now let me quote something that I have read from another Author that has helped me, and here it is, "A person who has only a rusty screwdriver with a will to do what God wants them to do… will do more for God, than a person with a whole garage full of tools who won't do what God wants them to do." So, with a laptop and the will to do what God wanted me to, I wrote my first book, then my second, and now a third!

They will soon be available on Amazon! Check them out and share them with family and/or friends that need to meet and experience Jesus as I have. My books, "Be The Moon, Reflect the Sun," "Older Than 6000," and "Time Is Running Out," will reach people through their minds, their intellect, and their hearts! Love you, friends!

12

FROM IRELANDS SHORES

KAREN BORELAND

The beautiful Island of Ireland is known for its 40 Shades of Green. Why is that, you say? As you travel the countryside with its many fields, valleys and glens, there's a lush beauty of many colors unmatched anywhere. There, a young boy was born to a family who lived in the capital city of Belfast in the north of Ireland, part of the United Kingdom. His name was Jimmy Boreland. There was an older sister Elizabeth, who was affectionately called Lily by her family, and an older brother, Bobby, Robert. They lived on Northland Street, off Shankill Road, one of the main boulevards leading north out of the city.

Tragedy struck when Jimmy was only four years of age. His father worked at Harland and Wolff, where the Titanic was built, the second largest shipbuilding works in the world at the time, second only to Glasgow, Scotland. Daily he went to work at that large firm in the Port of Belfast. On this horrible day, word came that Mr. Boreland had been killed in a work-related accident. It left the family reeling from the news. By this time, Jimmy had a younger brother George and an infant brother who had recently been born. Because of the trauma caused by the death of her husband, mother Mary, whom they called May, could not sufficiently nourish the baby with her milk causing baby John to pass away shortly after that.

Several years later, Germany ravaged much of Europe with destruction, hunger, and death in World War II. As fate would have it, the United Kingdom became involved in the war effort. The German Luftwaffe planes began bombing London and Belfast, which devastated people's lives, killing many and destroying homes, businesses, and factories in the cities. Air raid shelters were built throughout the cities for people to run to for safety and protection when the sirens rang out, warning of bombers approaching. It became clear that when shelters got direct hits, they needed to evacuate the children to country farms to save the next generation.

The three young Boreland boys were moved to Mrs. Michael's farm in the country far north of Belfast in the village of Aghadowey (pronounced AWK-A-DUE-EE) just south of the northern coastal town of Portstewart and the city of Coleraine. Consequently, it was very traumatic for all the children to be uprooted from family and friends. It helped to calm them when mothers would visit the farms once a month, but many tears were shed again at the parting of parents' visits. After a few months, Jimmy's older brother Bobby was allowed to return home with his mother to the city of Belfast.

On the farm, Jimmy was fascinated with all the animals, so one day he was admiring the horses. A farmhand asked him if he would like to sit on one of the horses, and Jimmy gladly accepted the invitation. Wow, a city boy getting to sit on a horse, what a thrill. He lifted the boy up and set him there with no saddle, just the man to take hold of, then the unthinkable happened. The farmhand struck the horse's hindquarters causing the animal to lunge forward, and young Jimmy fell off and landed hard on his left arm.

Immediately, his arm swelled way up under his twisted jacket sleeve. He was taken to the nearest hospital; the x-rays showed a fractured wrist. Now, with the cast on his arm, much rest, and a short hospital stay, he was taken back to the farm. He never told Mrs. Michael what her farmhand had actually done to cause his accident.

After two years, the war ended, with Britain and America as strong allies. Life in Europe was at peace, and countries began rebuilding. By this time, May had moved to Canmore Street off Shankill Road to a bigger place. The Boreland boys were reunited with family, saw their friends, and started back to school in their own neighborhoods. May would send the boys to Sunday School every week to the Assembly of God church down the street. Occasionally they would go to the Salvation Army Sunday School close by also.

As Jimmy grew, he was the leader of his own little mischievous gang. He had his way of getting his members to steal comic books and candy bars. For example, he would tell the other members to give Tommy the silent treatment until he would do what he was told to do. That's how Jimmy ran his operation. The gang would go in and distract the owner while Tommy would put the comics and/or candy in his jacket. Then they would leave and enjoy the fare at their favorite hangout spot.

With no father in the house, May had to work long hours to support her family. When the boys finished the Eighth Standard in public school, rather than going to university, she insisted they go to work and help with the financial burden of the household. Factories had long hours from 8:00 a.m. to 6:00 p.m. Jimmy worked in various jobs; at one time, he was a damask weaver in the local linen factory.

Since he had no father, by the time he was seventeen, he had become extremely close to his older brother. Bobby had been attending a neighborhood church and had accepted Jesus as his personal Savior. A guest speaker was coming on a Friday night soon, and Bobby invited Jimmy to go with him on that particular night. Jimmy was not interested in going, but Bobby kept asking him, so to get rid of him, he said he would go. That night finally came, and Bobby told Jimmy to get ready for the special service.

He did NOT want to go at all, but he was always taught to keep his word. So, he turned to Bobby, shook his finger at him, and said, "Alright, I'll go but don't you think I'm going to get saved!" Sure, to his word, he did not yield to God that night. It was only a few weeks before Jimmy surrendered his life to The Lord and became a Christian.

In their upper teens and early 20s, they had a musical team that traveled around to various churches preaching, singing, and playing their accordions in special weekend meetings. Bobby, Jimmy, and Jackie Houston preached, sang, and played instruments. Their leader was Tommy Wardle, who had accommodations for the boys to travel, because Tommy's father owned the local fireplace shop. They did this for several years.

The opportunity came for Jimmy to attend Donald Gee's school, the International Bible Training Institute (IBTI) in Sussex, England, to prepare for the ministry and follow his call from The Lord. After he had been training for some time, his mother sent word that she needed him at home. His training ended then, and he was never able to return to Bible school.

Years passed for Jimmy, and now a young man of 24 years of age, he was to follow his brother, who had ventured to America six months before Jimmy's planned trip. It was nearing the time to confirm his itinerary with the payment at the travel office in

Belfast. Brother Bobby was supposed to send him the $300 provided by the sponsoring church in Long Beach, California. But he waited and waited for the mail to arrive from the United States, but it never came.

Jimmy Boreland was hard-pressed for the British Pound notes to pay for the tickets required for his travel. Time was fast approaching to confirm and pay his travel agent. He remembered another young man he knew who was going to New York City on the same date, so he contacted him and told him about his predicament, waiting to hear from his brother. His friend said that Jimmy should "ask the leadership of my church for the loan of funds and explain to them why to see if they would loan him the money for his trip. That he did, and they helped him to pay for his tickets in time for the deadline for payment with the ticket office.

October 1956 arrived, and it was time to pack his bag and a large suitcase because he had applied for a "permanent resident" status at the United States consulate. Finally, he was prepared for the long journey ahead. First, the ferry from Belfast to Black Pool, England; secondly, the long train ride from Black Pool to Southampton. When he was on the train south, he had what seemed to be a painful attack on his kidneys, and upon arrival, he was rushed to emergency at the local hospital.

Thankfully, there was enough time after his treatment to continue to the Southampton docks to board the Gurnard Lines ship for New York. Yes, this was a long, daunting journey to America. At that time, it was less expensive to travel by ship than to fly. All went well for the first seven days at sea on the nine-day passage. Ships only sway a little, typically. However, it was the end of October with probably not the best weather conditions, and Jimmy started getting seasick! His last two days of the nine days were miserable, to say the least.

After passing through customs in the New York City harbor, he said goodbye to his friend from Belfast, who was on his way to Canada. Jimmy then went on to the airport, later named JFK International Airport, to catch his flight to Los Angeles, California. He was so anticipating seeing Bobby upon his arrival.

After all, it had been six months since seeing his older brother. What? You mean Bobby is nowhere to be seen? He once again waited and waited (not only for the funds in Belfast for his trip). Now, he is waiting for Bobby to show up at LAX, as planned. He sat on his huge suitcase thinking... Now, what should he do?

He remembered the church in Long Beach where Bobby had been a guest speaker and had secured Jimmy's sponsorship for permanent residency by Pastor O. C. Harms. Well, he asked a cabby how much it would cost to ride to Long Beach, $10. That left him with only $2 in his wallet! He had the address of the elderly lady where Bobby was a guest during his preaching engagement at the church. He gave it to the taxi driver, and off they went. It was after midnight when he was dropped off. He knocked on the little lady's front door, hoping she would answer. Fortunately, she awoke and peeked out through the screen door. He asked for Bobby, and the parishioner said he wasn't there.

By now, it was 2:00 a.m., and wandering the streets of Long Beach certainly was not the recommended thing to do. Down at the corner was a church, and it just so happened that a light was flickering through one of the side windows. He knocked and was asked who he was. It was the assistant pastor, and when he heard Jimmy's thick Irish accent, he gladly let him in. He just happened to be preparing for a message he was to give for an upcoming meeting. He told Jimmy that it was extremely rare that he would be at the church at this time of night! Would you say it was providence? Yes, God watches after His children. It was meant to be that particular night!

The church had guest quarters, and Jimmy was allowed to stay there until his brother Bobby could come for him. By the way, where was Bobby? After asking the pastor that, he was told that Bobby had gone to Portland, Oregon, to see his pastor friend Dick Iverson who had previously ministered in meetings in Belfast. Bobby didn't know that Jimmy was actually coming from Northern Ireland since he had never sent the money for his fare to the U.S. That's why he wasn't at Los Angeles International Airport to get Jimmy when he arrived on October 30, 1956. After Jimmy called Pastor Iverson, Bobby drove to California to get Jimmy.

This was the beginning of the Boreland brothers' ministry in America, known as The Irish Gospelaires. More of our story will be in our upcoming book, From Irelands Shores.

13

LEARNING TO SPEAK AGAIN THROUGH NURSERY RHYMES AND RIGHT-BRAIN ART

DARRIN KISSINGER AND DIANE KISSINGER

I was 30 years old in June 1998 when I was packing for my first yearly two-week duty in the Naval Reserve as a Storekeeper third class and ran into some difficulties. I couldn't find my military identification, so the commander made me do extra work. I showed up late to hazardous materials school and ended up failing. My work aboard the ship was too slow, and I got put on kitchen patrol.

I actually liked food service work, but some days the food they gave us was barely edible. Putting out lots of ice-cold water was all I could do. People tried to keep hydrated in the extreme heat while mosquitoes buzzed around them. I wasn't too surprised that some people were throwing up, having high fevers, and put into quarantine.

I participated in tear gas and attack training among the many other activities. The tear gas trainers took it easy on my group but made others take off their masks for thirty seconds to experience the tear gas. Our group should have won our attack training match, but the other team's best sailor was allowed to continue fighting after being shot.

I made it through the two weeks and got ready to return home. Everyone moved out of their single rooms and roomed together for the last night. My new roommate said the doctors had just released him from quarantine, where he had been throwing up with a high fever, but he said he'd recovered. At the time, I wondered if he still had the fever because he kept the room extremely cold.

After flying home to Sacramento, I felt too tired to make it to the starting point of a bike trip I planned to go on, so I decided to rest and meet the group in Santa Cruz the next day. I met up with the biking group, but my health started deteriorating rapidly, and I returned to Sacramento.

I checked into a Sacramento Air Force base motel to quarantine and went to the base's clinic each day. I should have gone to a hospital emergency room, but I was afraid of getting a massive bill since I didn't have health insurance at the time. I also thought the clinic doctors would send me to an emergency room if I had a life-threatening issue.

After a few days at the base, I had a severe fever, was throwing up, and became delusional. Oddly, the doctors were very encouraging instead of being alarmed and said, "You are still alive. Keep on going! Good job!" They didn't give me any medicine or send me to a hospital. I felt helpless as I wasn't thinking clearly enough to call 911 to get to an emergency room on my own.

I kept throwing up. I would watch my thermometer, and my temperature kept increasing. My fever hit 107 degrees at one point. When a fever reaches 107 degrees, a person's brain begins to deteriorate, the fever starts destroying brain cells. Fortunately, my fever broke, and I began to think clearly again. I decided I better get to a private physician.

When I got to the private doctor, my temperature was 102 degrees. He was amazed that I survived the illness without medication and said my fever was reducing. He gave me ibuprofen, which I was to take until my temperature was back to normal, and told me to rest. I went to my parent's place to recuperate, and after resting for a week, I started feeling more like myself.

I decided I was healthy enough to travel to Athens, Georgia, for the two more weeks of storekeeper training I had requested. I went to my local Naval Reserve personnel office and asked if the commander had approved the tour of duty. The personnel guy said he had not reviewed it yet, but everything was three months behind, so I should go anyway.

Not having official orders meant I could not stay on base the first week. Somehow they made an exception for the second week. Everything seemed fine until I took the second of a series of three hepatitis vaccine shots. I can only assume my immune system went into overload, and I had not fully recovered from my first illness. My headaches and delusions returned. I tried to keep attending classes and keep a low profile till they passed. Unfortunately, I had already volunteered to pick a restaurant for our class party. The officer in charge asked for my suggestion, and I made an expensive recommendation. He was furious, took me outside, and reprimanded me. I couldn't handle it. I passed out, and the officer told a classmate to take me to the clinic on base.

I lost consciousness at the clinic, and the doctor believed I was in a psychiatric emergency. I was transported by ambulance to a local hospital emergency room, where they kept me under observation. I woke up but was still weak, delusional, and paranoid. Looking around, I saw my blood going into my IV and buzzed the nurse. For a moment, I thought I was going to bleed to death. Soon, though, the nurse arrived and fixed the IV. After a few more hours, the doctors discharged me and told me to drive to an Army psychiatric hospital the next day.

Still not recovered, I gripped the steering wheel and stared at the highway as I drove an hour to the hospital. They gave me a three-page form to fill out, but I couldn't focus on it. I took 30 minutes to fill it out. When the psychiatrists examined me, they asked why I took so long to fill out the form. After an hour of interrogation, my brain woke up, and I answered their questions to their satisfaction. Simultaneously, the hospital administrative staff told the doctors I had no approved training orders, and the doctors let me go. I flew home to my parents' house, running a high fever.

I arrived home a few hours before my parents left for a weekend vacation. Before departing, they walked to my room and found me staring out the window at the sun. I couldn't speak, so I just waved goodbye. I rested and tried to recover like before, but the delusions did not go away. When my parents returned, I was practically mute. My brain wasn't functioning, and I walked by, following my Mom around the house.

My parents took me to doctors, but they couldn't figure out what was wrong with me. I started hiking a lot during the day, and my parents were concerned. They placed me on a 72-hour hold in a county psychiatric ward that looked and felt like a horror film. It was dark and eerie looking. I was shown a small bare room with a bed with white sheets where I was to sleep. The psychiatrist gave everyone the antipsychotic medication Haldol, which caused many people to pass out on the floor. I figured out the Haldol made them so lethargic, and I didn't want to end up on the floor with them. When the nurse gave me the Haldol, I pretended to swallow the pills but actually hid them in my cheek. I spit them in the trash after he left.

Learning To Speak Again Through Nursery Rhymes and Ri... 89

Since I was scared of the place, I found a hole in the fence the next day and escaped through it. A half-hour later, a policeman found me hiking and drove me back to the facility. I endured one more day and was thrilled to return home after enduring three days in the psych ward.

Since I was still trying to understand God, I signed up for Bible School. Unfortunately, after a month, the dean asked to meet my parents despite completing the homework and passing the quizzes. He told them I couldn't stay in school because I couldn't interact with the teachers and students since I was mute. He also commented that I sat up straight all the time. I was confused and embarrassed. I'd never heard of anyone getting kicked out of school for being mute and sitting up straight. My parents were upset, too.

My parents and I continued to visit many different doctors, but there was little to no improvement in my condition. My Mom decided to use her teaching skills to stimulate my right brain. If she could do that, she thought, I could bridge the gap to my left brain and start to talk. So, whenever we would drive somewhere, my Mom would sing to me. Since my Mom was an elementary school teacher, she knew many nursery rhymes and sang them all to me. After another doctor's visit, she sang, "Yankee Doodle went to town riding on a ..." She stopped to take a breath, and I said, "pony." She looked at me in disbelief and began singing again. She again sang, "Yankee Doodle went to ..." and I said the word "town." She sang, "Yankee Doodle went to ..." over and over again, and each time, I would add "town."

I was talking! She chuckled, and I laughed too. Singing had connected my left brain to my right brain. My creative mind was starting to work again. My Mom was helping me to bridge the gap between singing and speaking. Going to church became a lot of fun because I could sing along with all the hymns and music. I even joined the choir. On a Sunday, we would often go to two or three church services because I loved singing, and my parents liked to encourage me. Nevertheless, I still couldn't communicate normally without the help of a song. Scientists say singing and speaking originate from different parts of the brain.

At the time, I loved the Bible, so my Mom read it to me. I wanted to memorize it, so she would read a verse, and I would try to draw it. She re-taught me essential art skills: circles, dots, straight lines, curved lines, and dotted lines. Stick figures for people were good enough for me. When I looked at my simplistic drawings, I remembered the Bible verse. I enjoyed drawing the verses, and things were starting to look up.

Mom happened to take a workshop from Betty Edwards, an excellent right-brain author, and artist. When my Mom learned about right-brain art, it seemed like the perfect next step for me. We began by drawing the side of a person's face. Then, we traced the silhouette of the first drawing as a mirror image. We always had to draw the person looking in the mirror. I could easily do that.

We progressed from drawing silhouettes to drawing simple coloring book pictures upside down. Most right-brained drawing is simply looking at a picture when the picture is turned upside down and drawing it. I would look at the lines, curves, and circles before noticing what the picture was, and then I used my creative mind to sketch them. Now I could sing and draw.

To make up for Bible school, I decided to read books from the library. When I could not find any more books I liked, I went to another library. Slowly, I began to talk about what I had learned. I seemed to be more capable of talking after eating a grilled salmon dinner my dad would make. Perhaps it was the Omega 3 in the fish. At a 1998 Christmas play, a kind man took an interest in me and listened to the few sentences I could string together as I slowly told him what I'd been doing. My right brain was connecting to my left brain, and I began to speak again.

My ability to speak gave me a lot of hope. Unfortunately, I also used it to voice a lot of pent-up frustration to my parents. It became too much for them, and they once again put me in the hospital for supervision and evaluation. My family visited me daily, and the staff was very kind. They did want to force me to take a shot of psychotropic medication, and I refused. I had a hearing in front of a judge. My mind was sharp as I defended my rights with excellent arguments using my new speaking ability. The judge decided I didn't have to take the shot. I was very relieved.

I wanted to sharpen my mind further, so I took various community college courses like chemistry, Spanish, guitar, psychology, and college success. I enjoyed being with other students and engaging my mind. I used these courses to re-engage with the world. I used them as a stepping stone to attend philosophy courses at Sacramento State University the following semester. I would graduate from the community college in 2000 with an associate degree.

God gave me a second life. I recovered from the high fever that caused me to be mute. I have continued learning and sharing with others, even though it has been difficult. Despite the fever that almost robbed me of my brain and my life, I ended up getting my Masters Degree in Practical Theology. I'm now working towards my Ph.D., when about twenty years ago, I was kicked out of Bible school, singing nursery rhymes and drawing simple shapes and curves.

Throughout my recovery, my parents and I have prayed for the Lord to help us be a source of light, love, and joy for others. We are thankful for my healing, and we pray that the story of my recovery and dedication to learning will inspire others. We thank the Lord, for He is the eternal source of love and joy. Even when circumstances seem hopeless, He can restore life and make us ready to fulfill our purpose.

14

STATE OF SHOCK

JEANA SHACKELFORD

July 28th, 2018, was the day my life was forever changed. I was at a weightlifting clinic with friends from my gym when I saw an incoming call. I felt a bit of panic seeing my mother calling. She knew I was busy that day. We were on a short water break, so I answered. I noticed the tone of her voice immediately; she seemed rushed and frantic. Next, I heard her say, "There has been an accident, you need to come home. Your brother wrecked his motorcycle."

My heart started pounding, and my mind began to race. I hung up the phone and looked up to find my friends looking on with obvious concern. I told them I had to leave. Something had happened to my brother, gathered up my things quickly, and tore out of the parking lot. I was all the way in Tulsa and heading towards Mannford using every shortcut I could remember. My mind continued to race, running through all the scenarios and planning what to do when I arrived.

My brother, a truck driver, was in town for the weekend, and his kids were at my parent's house for a visit, so I envisioned myself staying with the kids and letting my parents go to the hospital while everything got figured out. This thirty-minute drive seemed to last forever, and then finally, I could make out the sign that was the road to my parent's home.

Pulling off the highway, I thought of the last time he wrecked his bike, how we all yelled at him for not wearing a helmet, and then feeling thankful it was not any worse. I saw flashing lights coming up on the big curve in the road. Then I noticed a line of cars pulled off to the side of the road, and I recognized one of the cars was some long-time family friends that lived a couple of doors down. Then I saw their other car parked behind the first, I kept driving and saw both my parent's cars too.

I was surprised to see my family waving to a police officer and me motioning for me to park my car behind the others. I was so confused as to why no one seemed to be in a hurry. As I was getting out of my car, I saw my mother. I saw her eyes. I knew something was very wrong as she had been crying. She came over to me and softly said, "He is gone, we lost him."

All the breath in my lungs rushed out at once, and my world went dark. It felt like the earth had fallen from my feet, and every piece of my body was experiencing sharp stabbing pains. Intense bouts of rage followed floods of tears. I yelled. I screamed. I punched my car and was shocked at how numb my hands felt. We stood in that ditch for what seemed to like days.

We had to wait for the coroner to show up, and no one was about to leave him there. So, we waited in the hottest part of the day. My father had just had knee replacement surgery and was balancing on a cane. No matter who urged him to sit, that was not happening. After some coaxing, we pulled his truck a bit closer and sat on the tailgate. We watched as they calculated the trajectory of my brother's motorcycle exiting the roadway and entering the ravine. They measured the tire tread on the ground, checked to see if he used the brakes, and continued to fill out their reports. I couldn't help but think what an awful job that must be and then doing it in front of our grieving family; they were so respectful and courteous.

Each car that passed fueled such fury. They slowly drove by, looking at us and trying to see what had happened. We had neighbors stop and ask about what was going on! I wanted to scream at every single one of them. How could they not know that someone has just died? How could they not see that we were utterly broken people standing on the side of the road? It felt like all our pain was on display for every passerby. They could have had genuine concern in their hearts, but I could not see it at that moment. If you see people on the side of the road, I urge you to try your best not to rubber neck. These are the worst moments of their lives, and the last thing they need is to feel like entertainment.

My eyes would run across the tarp on the ground every few moments. I could see a very still shape just underneath. I wanted them to all be wrong. I wanted to see him move. I prayed over and over for him to move and get up, saying this had all been a horrible joke. The longer he was still, the more reality set in. I asked him, "How could you leave me?" I began to realize I have never lived in this world without him. I could not believe that under that tarp lay the body of my best friend. My person. My brother!

My brother and I had such a special bond. We could have whole conversations across a crowded room and never say a word, and it used to infuriate people. We had a way of understanding each other in a way only the closest siblings know. I watched the sweat roll down my legs when the coroner made his way to the scene. He pulled up and parked, and the officers made their way to him. I kept replaying a phone call from just a few hours before.

My brother had called me and said he and the kids would be at my parents' house, so I should come by and have dinner. We talked for a few minutes, and I told him I would be there and asked what he was doing. He told me he had been out riding his bike and would meet up with a friend and head out to Mannford. We made plans; I was going right over there after we got finished with this clinic at the gym. He called me a few names, and I called him an idiot. We laughed and said, "See you later; love you."

My parents moved around me and said we should go home now. They were starting to get him loaded up, and they did not want me to watch. I kept thinking, how could this be real? We just made plans. His voice echoed in my mind. Pulling up to the house, his truck came into view. A huge red semi-truck he shared with his best bud sat in the driveway. They were a driving team, and they had plans too. I thought of his friend and how he must have been devastated as well. Again, rage took over me, and I punched his truck over and over. I dreaded seeing the kids. As much as I was hurting, I could not imagine what they must have been feeling.

We made our way inside and hugged. We cried. We sat in silence. Suddenly I had the urge to smoke a cigarette and make a drink; I quit smoking a couple of years back. I sat on the porch as family filtered in and out, coming to show their love and support. It felt like I was underwater, watching everything transpire, yet just under the surface. Sounds were muffled, my vision was hazy, and I began to lose track of whole days and time altogether.

Nightfall would come, and that tarp would haunt my mind. I would close my eyes in the middle of the day and see that damn tarp. It was everywhere. As we made the arrangements for my brother's funeral, at the last minute, I posted a call out for bikers to come and escort him to one more party, the VFW out in Mannford.

The day came that we had all wanted to skip over. Pulling into the funeral home, I saw cars parked everywhere and huge line of bikes waiting. I cannot even explain what it meant to see those bikes. It brings tears to my eyes every time I think about it. As we made our way inside to wait, we navigated around so many people. More than 300 people showed up to pay their respects to my brother and our family. We looked on as people in suits rubbed elbows with people decked out in leather from all walks of life present that day. I was in awe at how many people my brother had touched in his short 35 years and how much love poured in from so many places. I just had no idea what was in store for me in the next few days, and looking back, how could I have known?

15

FEAR AND LOVE

BRYAN SIMS

Psychiatrists, psychologists, spiritual gurus, and religious zealots the world over have tried to construct an answer to this problem, this affliction, the stumbling block called fear. Some call fear and emotion, and others call it an energy field; the Bible calls it a spirit (2 Tim. 1:7). Fear controls much of the world. In most cases, it works in a very subtle way, but at times we see it rampaging through society. Fear can operate in such a subdued manner that it can manipulate a person and frequently goes unnoticed. Other times it grips the mind and tries to smother the person's will. In any case, it must not be tolerated.

So, what do we do? First, let's look at it straight on, size it up, and examine its many nuances. Let's look at some manifestations of fear to know what we're dealing with. Unfortunately, most people have very little understanding of anxiety. Most people think that fear is just panic or fright. These are outward graphic manifestations of fear, but many other overlooked types of fear exist. To get a somewhat in-depth look at this subject, let's start at the beginning.

Where did fear originate? Fear originated with Lucifer (Isa. 14:12-17; Eze. 28:13-19). The Bible says that Lucifer, now Satan, rebelled against God and tried to exalt himself to God's level. Iniquity was found in him, and he was full of pride. Here we see that fear started with Lucifer. He was unsatisfied with his position, and because of pride, he fell from his place with God (Pro. 16:18; Eze. 28:17; Luke 10:18).

Pride is a manifestation of fear. A person is insecure or fearful of how others view them. They exalt themselves to try and feel better and look better to others. Pride or ego-consciousness works hard to impress people because it's afraid of appearing inferior or rejected (Pro. 16:18, 29:23, etc.).

Another fear we can analyze is strife. Strife is fanned by fear-based anger resulting in conflict. It struggles for superiority. Strife is afraid of losing its position or possessions. Strife can rise when control is lost (Pro. 17:14,19, 26:20-24; James 3:16). Strife and pride go together (Pro. 13:10, 28:25). Prideful people always have a propensity for strife or discord.

The next fear we will study is greed. Greed or hoarding is fear-based. It is a fear of never having enough or losing what you have. It also manifests in trying to obtain more than others have (Pro. 1:19, 15:27). Proverbs 1:19 is, in fact, an interesting paradox in being greedy for gain. As the verse says, the person's life gets taken away. A rapacious attitude will cause one to lose their life in some measure.

The next fear we will investigate is a severe and replete fear that dominates our society today: the fear of being offended. We live in a society that is insecure, angry and hurt most of the time. This is a fear of vast boundless proportions. Being offended or offense comes about by being angry about not getting your way. It also comes from being overly concerned with what others think and say about us. Whatever offends you weakens you through fear. It often escalates into strife and bitterness. (Pro. 18:19; Matt. 11:6; James 3:2). Pride is also at work with this fear. Eleanor Roosevelt said, "No one can make us feel inferior without our permission." Fear always runs side by side, so to speak, with selfishness. We all grapple with this affliction, afraid that we won't get our way, being concerned only with our wants and needs. We should undoubtedly love ourselves, but selfish people focus on themselves to the point that it produces pressure, with minimal regard for others.

According to the Bible, all fear known to man can be traced back to the fear of death (Heb. 2:14, 15). The fear of death is the master fear; it supports all others. This, of course, is not an exhaustive list, but you are gaining a broader view of what fear is and how it functions. Let's continue to look at fear and how it operates. If you examine any problem, you will find that at the root of it is fear. There are undoubtedly other components to the anatomy of a problem depending on how deeply involved or far-reaching it is; however, fear is at its heart.

Here are three examples that I have used in sermons to illustrate what I'm trying to convey. First, a young woman works around the clock to keep the doors open at her small business. Sales are down, the bills are piling up, and her staff needs to be paid. She's coping with a sluggish economy and doesn't know what to do. Second, a teenage boy has gotten involved with the wrong crowd. He's out late running the streets, wreaking havoc, and coming home smelling of alcohol. His parents have tried to discipline him but to no avail. They don't know what to do. Third, a couple has been arguing and continually fighting over the past few years. The problems just aren't getting resolved. They question their marriage's future and don't know which way to turn.

As you can see, here are three unique problems. Each predicament has its own set of circumstances, and there is wisdom for each situation. The commonality in each conflict is, you guessed it, dealing with fear. If the fear is not expunged, these problems will not cease. They will continue and most likely get worse. The spirit world is the real world. The natural world we contact with our five physical senses is a lower, slower spinoff or byproduct of the spirit's realm.

Faith and fear make everything work. Faith and fear are both spiritual forces going in the opposite direction. Faith in God connects us to God. It connects us to God's word, promises, and provision. On the other hand, fear ties a person to Satan and his destructive power. Fear is faith in death, destruction, and what's not desired. Laws construct the spirit world (Rom. 8:2). Faith or fear puts these laws into motion. Faith and fear are laws themselves. As an individual yields to them through entertaining thoughts, speaking words, or actions, faith or fear come to pass in a person's life (Job 3:25:26).

To a certain degree, we now see the magnitude, the scope of this dangerous far-reaching entity called fear. By now, you are undoubtedly asking, what is the answer to this diabolical oppressor? Fear must be continually resisted. It must be stopped (Ps. 118:6; 2 Cor. 10:3-5). God and Jesus repeatedly said, "fear not" (Isa. 7:4, 43:1,5; Luke 12:7; Rev. 1:17,18, etc.). We must also realize that we have been delivered from fear through Jesus finished work on the cross (Rom. 8:15, Heb. 2:14-15). More importantly, in God himself, the answer is love (1 John 4:8,16). When we receive Jesus as our savior, God's love is put in our hearts (Rom. 5:5). We can then love God (John 14:21,23; 1 John 4:19, 5:2,3) and receive his love (John 13:34, 15:9; 1 John 3:1, etc.). We must understand that perfect, mature, or complete love casts out fear. As we develop a relationship with God, the love inside our spirit matures and becomes perfect.

How does this process work? 1 John 2:5 says by keeping the Word (the Bible) perfects the love and doing what the Word of God says to do. Abiding in it and Him (John 15), forgiving people (Mark 11:25; Eph. 4:32), attending church (Heb. 10:25), developing a prayer life (Luke 10:18; Eph. 6:18, etc.), and reading and studying the Bible (2 Tim. 2:15, 3:16) are some examples. As we practice loving people, God's love is developed in us (John 13:34, 15:12; Eph. 5:1-2; 1 John 4:12). Deciding to know through study and meditation (Josh. 1:8; Ps. 1:2; 1 Tim. 4:15; 2 Tim. 2:15), and believe the love God has to us (John 15:9, 17:23-26; 1 John 3:1) will make a person strong and confident in their relationship with God.

It can be an arduous task to develop God's love if a person isn't sincere about their commitment. One must spend time in His Word and fellowship with God (Josh. 1:8; 2 Tim. 2:15). As a person does this, walking by faith (2 Cor. 5:7, etc.), and loving people, especially difficult people (Luke 6:7,35) will be possible. It will be attainable because we know in our hearts that almighty God loves us. Jesus loves us so much that He came and died in our place to bring us into the family of God (Isa. 53; Matt. 27; Mark 15; Luke 23; John 19). As we become strong in these truths, God's love is perfected or matured in the reborn human spirit. If we dare to believe it, 1 John 4:17 says, "...as he is, so are we in this world." The strong, confident, developed believer walks like Jesus, talks like Jesus, and becomes, yes, like Jesus! What are the results of what happens when these things are accomplished? 1 John 4:18 says, "There is no fear in love; but perfect love casts out fear!" The developed mature believer is so full of God's love that there is no room for fear.

I started this chapter by writing that people of various disciplines worldwide have tried to overcome this problem of fear with little and, in many cases, no results. People have sought counselors, therapists, and psychiatrists and have taken medication, and have talked to their friends to overcome fear to no avail. The only thing that will eradicate fear is a relationship with Jesus and knowing the love of God intimately. A person must decide to love God with all their heart, soul, and mind, as Jesus said in Matthew 22:37. They must give themselves entirely over to him and make their life a life of love to God and others. Then that person will realize the reality of 1 John 4:18 (KJV), which says, "There is no fear in love, but perfect love casts out fear because of fear hath torment. He that feareth is not made perfect in love."

16

FINDING PEACE THROUGH TRAUMA

JILLIAN WILSON

I'm going to take you on a journey of self-discovery. The ups and downs along the way, and finding peace and my purpose!

I grew up in Oklahoma. I had a mom and a dad. I had three older siblings, cousins, aunts, and uncles. I was always the black sheep and never quite lived up to the expectations placed on me. But I always rebelled against what society wanted. It drove my family crazy. I know that because the things I was told growing up made me believe I was worthless and a nobody. I had an older sister that used to say horrible things to me. I truly believed she hated me. I didn't realize until I was an adult that she hated herself. She just wanted everyone else to feel like she did. It worked for a while, and now I know that it's ok not to like her as a person and love her from afar and hope that one day she steps out of fear and denial and looks at herself in the mirror, and realizes she needs to deal.

A pivotal point in my life that shook me to the core was when my mom died of cancer when I was 16. I had never imagined life without her until that point. I thought my mom was superhuman and would never die. I had never really been a party girl. I started going to parties, drinking myself drunk, and taking every drug offered to me to kill the pain of my heart ripping apart. But in the morning, I woke up with that same hole and emptiness. Like my heart was once again ripped out of my chest and stepped on. My dad moved me to a small town in Oklahoma, where he grew up. I hated that damn place. His family are some of the meanest, cruelest and pretentious people I've ever known. They look down on people like they are gods, and everyone else are ants that need squashing. I went to school every day, smiled, and played along as society expected, and I would party myself to sleep every night. I even had a boyfriend, but I never allowed him to get super close to me in any way.

I remember the night it happened so vividly, like it was a dream. But it wasn't any dream. It was the moment I realized just how screwed up this society is and how it sees women. I didn't realize how it would change everything and haunt me for years to come. It was February 1999, just about six weeks after my mom died. Myself and two of my girlfriends were invited to a party my boyfriend was going to. So, we decided to go. Why the hell not? It was just another party for me to kill the sucking void in my chest where my heart used to be.

We went and met everyone at the lake. We were partying on a rock cliff by a waterfall. There were way more guys than girls there. Actually, my two friends and I were the only girls there. Little did I know of the plan they had made for the night. A couple of the guys there had gotten into a car accident about a week before and were passing out their pain pills, but only to the guys. They refused to let us have any... yet. Later that night my boyfriend said he had to go home because he had to work the next day. He told me he wanted his letterman jacket and class ring that I wore around my neck because he didn't want them lost or ruined from the alcohol.

So even now, I thought it was weird that I gave them to him. Within a couple of hours, I was puking up alcohol from trying to drink the nasty beer that was available. One of the guys from the accident gave me a couple of pills. He said it would help. I decided I was done with partying and went up to one of the guy's Suburban and passed out. I remember waking up to someone tugging on me. When I opened my eyes, I realized I wasn't being tugged on. Some of the guys were trying to take off my pants. As I tried to get up to grab my pants, I realized how many were in the Suburban with me.

I was now being held down because I was trying to fight them off me. I started screaming for them to stop and for someone to help me. Trying to fight five guys off isn't an easy task. They ripped my clothes off, and placed their hands over my mouth. I could tell they were aggravated that it was no longer an easy lay. They took their turns taking what they wanted. It seemed to go on for hours. I'm guessing it was about 40 minutes of hell. I remember thinking, what did I ever do to deserve this, and why did I come to this stupid party?

After it was over, they threw me out of the suburban and threw my clothes at me. As they started to drive off and leave me there, someone said, "we can't leave her here." I was terrified to get back in, but I was in the middle of nowhere and had no idea how to get home. Reluctantly, after putting my clothes back on, I got in the back. I curled up in a ball and didn't move until we got to my block. I jumped out and ran to my house. After I locked the door behind me, I ran to the bathroom and took a shower. I scrubbed every inch of my body until I almost bled while sobbing in despair. How badly I wanted my mother at that moment. I tried to forget what had happened. I had told no one.

That Monday after the party, I got up and tried to pull myself together. Get my bag and get in my car, and head to school. School that day was another day of misery from hell.

My boyfriend walked up to me that morning and said I was a slut, and we were done. I tried to tell him that wasn't how it happened. He didn't want to hear it. They had been bragging all weekend about this awesome party. They made me out to be this awful person who slept with multiple guys. I couldn't believe I had become the villain. At one of my classes that afternoon, one of the guys came in bragging about the party, and I lost it and ran out crying.

My cousin's girlfriend ran out after me. She asked me what was wrong, and then I blurted out that he was lying and the party was horrible. She asked me what had happened. I eventually told her, and she was pissed. She couldn't believe I was blaming myself for their actions. I told her not to tell anyone, and she said ok. That day after school, she told my cousin. He was furious! He came over and told me he was going to kill those guys. I begged him to let it go, and I didn't want anything to happen to them. He said he would let it go if I told my dad.

So, as much as I didn't want to, I did. To this day, I struggle to have a relationship with my dad because of what he said and did after I told him. When I went to him, we were at my grandma's. I told him what had happened and he was mad at me for going to the party. My grandma also told me that I should not have gone. My aunt told me I got what I deserved for going, and that will teach me to do what I'm told. I ran out crying! I went somewhere quiet and cried in my car for what seemed like hours. Then I went home and locked myself in my room for the rest of the night.

The next day my dad got up and went to work. He never said a word to me since I had told him; he just ignored me. I decided that I couldn't live in that town anymore. I backed my car up to my bedroom window, packed my bags, and ran away. The whole drive to the city, I thought many times about driving my car off a bridge or into oncoming traffic. I thought it would be better if I didn't exist. I eventually got to one of my best friends' house. I kind of told her what happened. I stayed with her for a couple of days and hid out. Nobody knew where I was, and her mom said I had to go to a family's house and tell them what happened. So I chose to go to my brother and sister-in-law's house. I told my sister-in-law what had happened. My sister-in-law called one of my aunts to tell her where I was, and she came right over.

My aunt gets there and tells me that no matter what has happened, there is no excuse for running away. My sister-in-law told her she might want to sit down for this. I was looking down and didn't want to look up to tell her, so I closed my eyes as I started crying and told her what happened. I was expecting the same reaction my dad and his family had. She said, "Oh my God, Jill" and hugged me.

We live in a world where a child is told who they are and who they will be instead of letting them have their own journey and experiences. Society wants you to live by all of these expectations and rules inside of a box. Like the queen bee directing the worker bees. Have you ever taken a step back and watched people? Everyone appears to be on autopilot, like zombies. People have conformed to society and the incredibly small box of do's and dont's.

We have become a society that blames the victims. Society has made us believe that a person's looks determine their worth. That their looks determine their character, morals & ethics. We are so busy judging everyone else that we don't look inside ourselves at our flaws. Society has tried to keep us volatile and fighting each other instead of coming together.

Anytime a person has been sexually assaulted, they assume the victim did something wrong instead of blaming the person who committed the act. Why don't we hold the person committing this atrocity accountable for their actions? Why is it that they are superior and allowed to act so heinous? Yet, when a person is sexually assaulted, they are blamed for being the victim. I can tell you I didn't deserve it. I don't believe any person who has ever been sexually assaulted deserved it. We have to do better and be better!

Do we really want our children and grandchildren growing up believing they are worthless? That they are to blame for being sexually assaulted? We need to change. We need to teach our children their worth. We need to speak up. We need to let them know that we see them and that they are not alone. The statistics of sexual assault in the US are staggering and heartbreaking. 1 in 3 women will be sexually assaulted in their lifetime, and 1 in 6 men will be sexually assaulted in their lifetime. Everyone knows at least one person that has experienced this trauma. So today, please take a moment to let that sink in. Please help me fight back by letting your loved ones affected by this know they are worthy, and you see them, and they aren't alone. Together we can change!

17

WHY NOT ME?

JAVIER HERRERA

Why ME? Have you ever asked yourself this question? It's safe to say that we all have, but the beauty of that question is the one that comes after it. What NOW? That's the question I asked myself sitting in the Mall Parking lot in my car, tears rolling down my face as I felt defeated in all three aspects of my Life; Physically, Mentally, and Spiritually.

Why! Why me? I said after realizing I had lost everything my job, relationships, and businesses. I want to introduce myself. My name is Javier G. Herrera. I'm an artist, business enthusiast, investor, author, and professional communicator in the creative arts and sales, and I'm here to share with you a story. This story includes some relatable experiences and several simple life lessons. I'll show you how I overcame my challenges using a method I like to call The Process of the 4 "P's" to push through and create a better life.

Now, before I get to the 4 P's... I know you really want to know, but before I tell you my story, I want to ask you a question. Why do stories, in general, even matter? Well, storytelling is a powerful tool, and I genuinely believe a fundamental aspect of being who we are today as creative and intellectual human beings and what we were created for. It's a way to communicate in a much deeper way where we can teach each other important information, connect emotionally, and learn how to access compassion and empathy for one another—learning different perspectives from all around the world from different points of view that can be used to pass down knowledge and morals.

Now back to what I was saying, The 4 P's: Problem, Process, Perspective, and Passion.

This is how I took myself from being in a PROBLEM to PROCESSING my situation, which changed my PERSPECTIVE that led me to correct my PASSION which drove me to take ACTION!

The "Four P's" changed everything in my life, and I want to pass that on to whoever has been in a similar situation. I truly believe that if you take these steps and implement them as I did, your life can change too!

Problems can come in all sorts of shapes and forms. No one's problems are more significant than the others. Understanding that and having compassion towards others' problems is key to this process. Not looking at your friend, family, or neighbor's problem and mocking as if that's not an issue. We all come from different backgrounds, and all with different pasts. You have no idea what others have been through or overcome. But with proper communication and storytelling, you can unlock something powerful.

Viewing things this way will give you a new set of eyes, a new perspective, and newfound respect for one another. My problems five years ago resulted in losing my job, business, and relationship. This led me to face one of my biggest fears of all

DEBT. By the time I knew it, I was drowning in over 100K in debt, losing everything I had ever worked for. Shortly after I started feeling something I had never felt before. This thing called "Depression."

Now, let's go back to what I was saying. Never judge anyone's problems or situations; I used to believe that depression is just a type of mental weakness. My thoughts on this topic were very arrogant, and I always asked myself, "why don't they just read books on personal development?" "Why don't "they" as if "they" weren't people? Little did I know I would soon experience this dark season in my life. It happened so quickly yet slowly over time; it was as if I was sinking and drowning in quicksand. My perspective on depression would forever be changed.

Now, it's my goal to help others in this area overcome any issue or situation they feel they can't get out of. It is the power of loving one another as how you would want to be loved. Because at my lowest point, that is what helped me the most. Knowing that I was loved and that NO mistake, situation, or failure could ever change that.

The power of processing is powerful. What do I mean? Being able to process my situation and my PROBLEM at the time, I shifted and changed how I viewed and looked at things. Process as a verb, PRO-CESS, is to "walk or march in procession." You're moving forward from a situation or problem and not allowing yourself to sit and stay in one place or live in your past.

"There's a reason why the windshield is bigger than your rearview mirror!" My pastor said at a conference once, speaking on "The Process," the process we called life. Through this time of process, I was able to discover some things about myself. A few things I needed to explore and get some answers. Questions like "Who am I?" And "What is my destiny?"

Going through this process, I felt I was supposed to attend a three-year Bible College at my Church. I wasn't sure how I would pay my way through it, but I took a step of faith and didn't allow my situation or money to be a stop sign. Now I'm not saying that everyone needs to attend a Bible College, but I am saying that through my process, I was able to find those answers that I kept asking myself. I was also surrounding myself with a group of individuals speaking into my life and shifting my PERSPECTIVE. They were the support group that taught me where to search and how to read the Bible for important Kingdom principles and truth that I was able to build my life upon.

How we look at things can impact every decision we make. This means Perspective is critical in our daily life. That NEW perspective helped me through the toughest chapter of my life, and going through that process allowed me to view things differently. I was able to grow out of the old way of thinking and embrace this new mindset. My biggest fear, DEBT turned into my biggest strength; how you might ask. My biggest obstacle turned into my biggest opportunity, an opportunity to learn new skills on how to budget and live life at a low cost. Knowing I didn't need much to survive, I was content with what was needed, and having good friends are powerful.

If you replace what you fear the most with knowledge and awareness, you can create room to realize what actually matters in your life. I gave myself permission to discover my true desires and what brings joy and happiness into my life. PERSPECTIVE allowed me to see my true passions in life without focusing on my fears and masking them with what I thought I loved.

What moves people from being good to great? PASSION! What can help anyone overcome an obstacle that seems impossible? PASSION! My heart and desires were transformed through those struggling years.

What do your passions consist of? Are they your passions, or are they passions influenced by your fears? Looking back and reflecting, my passions were to be successful and be the first millionaire in my family. Not having to worry about money and having time and freedom.

My heart is to serve and be of value, helping others that have been in situations where they feel like they can't escape. Giving hope to the hopeless and educating those that might not fully understand the questions they might ask themselves. My newfound PASSION has driven me to take ACTION and overcome many obstacles I once felt were impossible.

Now the real question to you is, WHY NOT YOU? Your Story Matters, and someone in this world is waiting to hear your story to help encourage and bring them hope. Your greatest test can be your greatest Testimony! The next time you're tempted to ask yourself, "Why Me?" challenge yourself to change your perspective, seek out your purpose, then ask yourself...

..."Why Not Me?"

18

KEEP THE TARGET

THAIS GUILHERME

"For I know the plans I have for you, declares the Lord, plans to prosper you and not to harm you, plans to give you hope and a future." Jeremiah 29:11 (NIV)

This is one of my favorite verses in the Bible. Every time I read it, I feel encouraged. It's amazing to see how God guarantees His plans for us to have an excellent future full of hope. That is what He has planned for our lives; we need to keep the target and focus on Him. With so many distractions in the world we are living in today, it can be hard to be still and listen to what God is saying.

We often tend to let our emotions dominate us, which affects our minds, making us doubt what God really has for us. He created us to be more than conquerors, so we must keep our eyes fixed on Him. Every day we wake up, we need to remember that He is there to help and guide us. We cannot let our discouragement take care of our life. In his words, He says:

"fixing our eyes on Jesus, the pioneer, and perfecter of faith..."
Hebrews 12:2a

As we know, His plans are greater than we think for our future, but the question is: Am I fulfilling God's purpose for my life? What do I need to do to achieve what He has for me? You can hear and find the right direction by seeking God's guidance with wholehearted surrender, active faith, and action.

First, you need to define what you desire to achieve rather than just hoping that someday you will achieve "something." When you don't have a goal or direction, you have no boost to take action. Being clear about what you plan to achieve is very helpful. You change your mind to focus on the "how" rather than the "what." Taking action, even in the slightest way, on a daily basis progresses you toward your goals, and these actions can add up to significant results over time.

- Do you have a goal in life that you want to achieve?
- Where do you see yourself in the future?
- What steps will you have to take to get there?

Those questions always pop into our minds, but the real question is: What am I doing to get there?

I share all of this as a significant part of my own experiences. I always had a dream in my heart to work in a bank, but in my thoughts, I could not see any possibility of that. I came from a low-income family, was born and raised in a small town, studying in a public school all my life; with no resource financially, it could be somewhat impossible for me to go to college, obtain a degree to be able to work in a Financial Institution one day.

My dad immigrated to the United States when I was ten years old. My parents were having relationship problems, financial hardships, and three kids to take care of. He had to make that decision to be able to provide for the family. It was very hard for my brothers and me to see my dad go with no perspective of when he would return. But even at a young age, we knew God's plan would be good and better for us. My dad wouldn't be away from us for so long without reason.

"We know that God works all things together for the good of those who love Him, who are called according to His purpose." Romans 8:28

God is so amazing that two months after I finished high school in Brazil, the family immigration process was approved for my dad, so my brothers and I moved to the United States, Boston, MA. I was 18 years old. It was the right moment to move since I did not have the financial resources to attend college in Brazil. All of this happened through His goodness and mercy; He really knows the right time for everything.

Imagine a young girl arriving in another country, not knowing anything about the culture, people, and language. That girl was me. Everything was so new to me. It was the biggest challenge of my life. I remember the days walking down the street, at shopping malls, listening to people talking, and being so lost. I couldn't understand anything in English. I couldn't communicate with anyone without having someone to translate for me. I remember how frustrating it was for me.

Of course, I was thrilled to live in this amazing country, but I knew that I would have to overcome many challenges to achieve my goal and have the job I dreamed about. The first question I had in mind was, "Where Do I need to start?" My first step was to learn and gain fluency in English. So, within 30 days of living in the States, I began my journey by starting my action plan. I began taking English classes five days a week. I had to work hard to pay for all my living expenses and school. I did not have anyone to support me financially. I was living with my dad, but I had to pay for all my expenses. We even had to split the rent and groceries. I had to work in two different jobs to be able to pay for everything. I remember all those days; it was exhausting. I had to overcome tiredness, discouragement, and everything that would come against my plan of action.

There was a time when I did not have the money to pay for school, and I had to work extra hours at the coffee shop, where I would start at 4 am every day. I ended up working there for five years. But I knew that was temporary. I always had my dream job alive in my heart and mind. I was my own motivator. I dedicated many hours to studying and doing my homework while everyone was asleep. I was the one who didn't have the money to do anything because everything I was earning was to pay for expenses and school. I never had extra. Sometimes I was criticized by family members. They would say I was the one that never had the money for anything, and I was wasting my time going to school every day instead of working more to save money. Those words hurt me a lot. I felt alone without any encouragement. But I knew I was working towards my goal, all of the struggles and sleepless nights would not be forever. I had to pay the price and sacrifice a lot of things in my life.

I remember I would save all the coins I received daily from tips to go on vacation. That was the only extra money I had. It was tough. I had to always stay strong because I knew this was the process I had to go through to realize my heart's desire. The faith in my heart kept me alive. I always prayed, seeking God for wisdom, direction, and guidance. New doors of opportunity would open. I had many opportunities to study in a few different English schools in Boston-MA, and one of those opportunities was to study at Harvard University. There, I completed my intermediate English as a second language course. I would never have thought I could have this amazing opportunity one day. God does even more than what we think or ask for.

"Never doubt God's mighty power to work in you and accomplish all this. He will achieve infinitely more than your greatest request, your most unbelievable dream, and exceed your wildest imagination" Ephesians 3:20 (TPT)

It is very easy to lose focus nowadays. There are so many options out there, but if you really desire success in life, you cannot let the obstacles be bigger than your dream and desire. The difficulties cannot discourage you. A few things you can keep in mind when you start this process are:

- 1-Establish a goal to keep your focus.
- 2-Be ready to face opposition and difficulties along the road.
- 3-Be willing to pay the price.

Remember, Achievement does not come for free.

Success is knowing that the reward will not be achieved immediately or come overnight; it will take time, but it will all be worth it in the end.

> "Those who value the process enjoy growth."

We all know that setting goals are important, but we often don't realize how important they are as we continue to progress. Setting a goal does not have to be boring or discouraging. There are many benefits and advantages when you set goals to work towards.

The desire and dream God placed in your heart is also His desire, you have to do your part in taking action, and He will give you the grace you need to accomplish your goal.

Setting goals helps you align your focus and start setting new habits and behaviors, and it helps you sustain momentum in life. It will encourage you to keep going. In the end, you can't manage what you don't measure and can't improve upon something if you don't know what you are doing.

The benefit of setting goals is that it helps you choose where you want to go in life. By knowing precisely what you want to achieve and your desires, you know where you have to concentrate and put your efforts. You will also quickly remove distractions that can easily lead you astray.

A useful way of making goals more effective is to use SMART GOALS, which stands for:

S – Specific (or Significant).

M – Measurable (or Meaningful).

A – Attainable (or Action-Oriented).

R – Relevant (or Rewarding).

T – Time-bound (or Trackable)

When a goal is established, you can see how amazing and powerful the process is. You start thinking about your ideal future, and you find the motivation to turn your vision of this future into reality.

One thing we must remember as we head in the direction we are going: focusing on the goal is more important than speed. We climb one step at a time.

We have to enjoy the journey as we progress. When we don't skip any steps, we can trust and believe we are going in the right direction. As we progress, we are being transformed as we move towards the desired place - the future. I encourage you not to waste your time but to potentiate it.

After a few years of studying English, I thought I was ready to apply for a job at the bank. I applied online, but unfortunately, I could not pass the assessment. My English skills were not good enough. I was sad and disappointed but did not give up hope; instead, it motivated me to keep going. I was even more dedicated to my studies and focused on my target. I exceeded my expectations and enrolled in a college to take extra advanced English grammar and writing courses. I knew the courses would better prepare me to reach my goal.

With one more year of study, I returned to the website and applied for the job I wanted at the bank, and to my surprise, it worked out! But I decided to go above my exceptions one more time. I didn't sit around waiting to be called for the interview. I went to the bank in person and asked for the manager. When I met her, I introduced myself, and I shared my interest in the job position. She looked at me and responded: "I loved your attitude. Come in tomorrow for the interview." What a happy day! I was super excited. When the big day came, I passed the interview and was offered the job. In these joyous moments, I was so grateful for the process I had to go through.

Remember: There will be times that YOUR attitude will be more relevant than your skills. Go above and beyond.

After working for a few years at Bank of America, another amazing opportunity arose. I moved to another state and started a new career at Navy Federal Credit Union – the largest credit union in the world. I started as a teller inside a branch, and while working there, I was able to attend college. Within two years, I was able to work my way up into a higher position at the corporate building. That was another great opportunity I will never forget. This being said, today, I have been working at this incredible financial institution for over five years. It has been a great journey. Today I don't work inside the corporate office but in the comfort of my home office. My job is incredibly rewarding because I have the opportunity to offer support and help to branch employees around the world.

> "Many times, we limit what we can achieve."

We can always go above and beyond our wildest dream and desire. He is always there, ready to empower us by giving us the strength and wisdom we need. We just need to take the first step and keep moving forward.

Remember this; we can do all things through Christ who strengthens us.

You are not alone in this journey. God once spoke with Joshua, and today He is speaking to you: "Be strong and courageous. Do not be afraid; do not be discouraged, for the Lord your God will be with you wherever you go." Joshua 1:9

Choose to believe in yourself. You have great potential inside of you. Don't be mediocre, thinking all is well the way it is. Life can be better; you can improve your skills and knowledge to accomplish much more. Never settle for less. God is in control of your life, yes, but if you don't do your part, He will not be able to accomplish the full purpose and plans He has for your life.

> "Without God, life has no purpose, and without purpose, life has no meaning." - Rick Warren

What will be your first step toward your goal?

Remember: Maintain your eyes fixed on the target.

- Do not give up.

- Do not listen to thoughts that come against your plan of action.
- Be consistent.
- Dedicate yourself.
- Never lose faith.
- Do your best!!! Yes, you can do it.

19

FLYING BY FAITH

TINA ROBINSON

In this chapter, I invite you to a small portion of my journey of stories that I began journaling, praying, and seeking God in my desperate search for answers. Amid doubt and misunderstanding, God faithfully revealed Himself in ways that mended the broken pieces of my heart. The Lord met me right where I was as I was drowning in grief and sorrow. I couldn't see, but He opened my eyes. He showed me He was always there and never left or forsaken me. I couldn't hear, but He opened my ears, and The Holy Spirit began leading and guiding me. He showed me how He had taken care of my daddy and how he has taken care of me and will always take care of me. These stories are true and dear to my heart. While God is not the author of death or grief, He is the Chief Shepherd, bringing me to spiritual maturity.

As we walked towards the Intensive Care Unit, we all had a posture of assurance to draw strength from The Spring of Living Waters. Being led by a woman of great faith and dignity, we gathered together, surrounding our Patriarch with love, as the vital signs could be seen no more. It was around 4:30 a.m.

on that "Glad Morning," and I knew that our daycare parents would arrive at the daycare center at 6:00 am. My beautiful and loving mother looked me in the eyes and assured me that everything was going to be ok, and she encouraged me that I could do it. There was work to be done. I mustered up enough strength to go and open our Family childcare center as usual. Off I went, business as usual.

A few hours passed, and the children joyfully engaged in their daily routines. There was a knock at the door. I recalled the friendly face peering through the glass window as I approached the door. I opened the door, and a chipper voice rang out and said, "Well, hello there. Is Pastor Frank here? I just dropped by to see him." I couldn't utter a sound. Immediately, my knees buckled, and tears burst from my eyes. He said, "What's the matter?" I told him that Pastor Frank went home to be with The Lord this morning. I can still see his face of shock and sadness. As he turned to go, he was filled with compassion and prayers for our family and me. This was my reality. Dad was really gone.

Standing planted at the door, something said… Something? Just as quick as that came out of my mouth, my father's voice rang in my mind. Dad would say, "something said? What do you mean something said? You mean the Holy Spirit spoke to you" I'm smiling. It hasn't been 24 hours since he transitioned, and I can still hear dad's voice. The sweet Holy Spirit spoke to me in a gentle tone. It was so clear and compelling. The Holy Spirit said, "This is the way they will come looking for me. They will look for me and will not find me." The scripture reads,

John 7:34 (ESV) says, "You will seek me, and you will not find me. Where I am, you cannot come." Although Jesus spoke to the Jews about His ascension in this verse, He spoke crystal clear to me, and I quickly snapped out of my dazed and confused stare. I thought, what is this? Lord, what are you saying? What do you want me to do?

The days ahead were dreadful, and I had just entered into the process of grieving. There were so many things going on that I could not find the words to say at the time. So as the days were drawing near to lay my sweet daddy to rest, that's just what I did... no words. However, there was something in me holding on to the hopes of a Lazarus experience.

After the funeral and the hustle and bustle of picking out the mask of the day, my world had shrunk to the four walls of my bedroom. I didn't know what to do or who to trust. I was heartbroken and vulnerable. Searching, seeking, and blocking, I only wanted to hear three words. Daddy is back! My friends, I am just being transparent and sharing something real, my heart.

You see, depending on the mask of the day, I functioned the best that I could on the outside and then rushed home to slumber in my quarters. I did this until the masks weren't working any longer. They say an idle mind is the devil's playground and boy did he try to do a number on me. I would hear conniving death thoughts the enemy would slide in and how it would try to kill me. Thoughts like, "You're going to die like your father, or you're going to be just like your uncle Ross" What? Are you serious, you hell-bound thief? I served him notice that he is under my feet just as the bible says he is. (Genesis 3:15; Ephesians 1:21-22; Luke 10:17-19; Romans 16:20)

My uncle had been deceased for over 10 plus years. I cannot remember the last time that I even mentioned my uncle's name. You see, that's how slick the enemy is. He was bogging down my mind with all kinds of thoughts as I lay in bed day to day, smothered with sadness. My friend, you will know when the thief speaks to you because he will try to take you out.

The scripture says that the thief comes to steal, kill and destroy. The next portion of that scripture is where my Heavenly Father destroys the works of the evil one. It reads, I have come to give life and that they might have it more abundantly. That's how good our father is.

John 10:10 (ESV) says, "The thief comes only to steal and kill and destroy. I came that they may have life and have it more abundantly."

I began to cry out to God and speak life to myself. I began to pick up the blueprint of my life and build my faith with The Word of God. I knew that I could not make it without Jesus.

I had to get up! Life didn't stop for me. It kept on going.

Have you ever lost someone that you were extremely close to? I know the pain seems to be unbearable, but if you continue to get up every morning and put one foot in front of the other and allow God to lead you through your woes and guide you through the process of grieving until you birth His beautiful plan for your life; every void will be filled with his love. Nobody can do it but God.

Isaiah 40:31 (ESV), "But they who wait for the Lord shall renew their strength; they shall mount up with wings like eagles, they shall run and not be wear; they shall walk and not faint."

My bedroom became my nest. I did not want to go to the bathroom and definitely did not want to leave the house. God sent a humble servant, a willing vessel, to speak to me, and I believe that the Holy Spirit gave him the words to say to me. He said, "If you stay in that nest too long, God will tear that nest up!" I know that word was sent for me. I watched a video on how the mother eagle looks out for her young eaglet as it leaves the nest. The eaglet has to learn how to fly.

The mother eagle models how to fly with her enormous wings stretched out. She exudes great strength as she soars gracefully in the wind. She knows sets out to protect the eaglet while giving enough room for her young to grow and build its confidence to land on a good tree. Even though the whirlwind filled the air and challenged the eaglet, it couldn't turn back. It has to choose to fly. It had to conquer the woes and the pain of stretching out its wings and soar.

God wants us to trust him. He wants us to be honest with him and have a conversation with him, a relationship. There's nothing that we are going through or have gone through that The Lord Jesus does not understand. There is nothing too hard for God. He wants us to come to him and ask. God hurts whenever we do not ask him according to his greatness, not man.

1 John 5:14 (ESV), "And this is the confidence that we have toward him, that if we ask anything according to his will, he hears us."

Matthew 7:7-8 (ESV), "Ask and it will be given to you; seek, and you will find; knock, and it will be opened to you. For everyone who asks receives, and the one who seeks finds, and to the one who knocks, it will be opened."

My friend, with Christ, let's take this leap together and do some flying. Flying by Faith!

20

IT'S OK IF YOU'RE NOT THERE YET

KATIA MOTZEVA-GUTIERREZ

When I was a high school teenager, I had no goals in life. Growing up in Bulgaria, I didn't have caring teachers to guide me, and we had no career counselors to help us plan our future. My parents did not push me to study, so I spent most of my time watching TV and hanging out with my friends.

But don't judge me too harshly. Consider that the one and only time I saw my conversational English teacher was when he came to cuss out our class for using his students' stereo, which they had left in our classroom; my literature teacher hinted without subtlety that if I wanted to get a good grade in her class, my dad should help her daughter get into university (he worked as a professor at said university); that I skipped probably one-third of all my high school classes because I knew that our homeroom teacher would excuse our absences without a note anyway; and that despite all that, I still graduated with an above average GPA.

My years of being a couch potato and watching cable TV did one good thing for me; it helped me learn English. Even after "studying" it through high school and taking a year of private lessons afterward, I could still not pass the university entrance exam to study English philology. So, I applied for something fun instead, photography. Thankfully, I passed the entrance exams, and I'm grateful I had a good eye for composition because even though my camera knowledge extended to pressing down a button, the professors liked my photos enough to let me into the program anyway. For the first time, I picked my own classes and enjoyed being in most of them. I even studied for my exams!

During my freshman year at university, my parents moved to the US after my dad got a job teaching at a Christian college in Washington state. This also made it possible for me to finish my education there, so on September 15, 2005, before the start of my sophomore year, I crossed the ocean blue to live in a tiny college town where I enrolled in a bachelor's degree in graphic design (they only offered photography as a minor).

American education was different. The university system, with its fifty-minute classes and endless homework assignments, reminded me more of high school than college (Bulgarian university classes are taught in blocks, and your final exams determine ninety percent of your class grade). And I was surprised to see that some of my teachers actually seemed to care about me. My photography and art professors in Bulgaria acted as though we were lucky to be in the same room as them. They had talked down to us and yelled at us (one time, I cried on my way home because I was shouted at for color grading my photos when I clearly "had no clue what I was doing").

Even though I did well academically, I was unprepared for culture shock, running me over like a freight train. I was a big-city girl living in a town with one traffic light. I was an introvert who did not know anyone and had left behind all her friends. I struggled with English prepositions (hang "out," hang "up," hang "on," seriously?!) and word pronunciation (I mean, who cares whether I wore ear mufflers or ear muffs, or whether my hair was shading or shedding?) which my new "friends" found hilarious (I am still sensitive about my spelling and make it a point to double-check everything I type). As an eastern European, I didn't understand why people acted so polite and friendly but were so uncomfortable about being touched and anyone invading their personal space.

Two years later, I was a straight-A student who was lonely, with no real friends, with a recently broken heart and drowning in a life devoid of purpose and meaning. In my desperation, I did the only thing I had the strength left to do... I turned to God and decided to change my major. On a cold and gloomy January day, I headed to the theology department because where better to find a way to crawl out of my pit of despair?

Since I switched majors in the middle of the school year, I could not join any bible language classes until the following fall. That left me in the small living room of a kind, retired, seventy-year-old professor who still taught languages for the university. During my first class of Modern Standard Arabic, he declared: "I claim you for the world of biblical scholarship!" He was my first mentor who took the time to teach me the ABCs of learning a language (what's a noun, what's an adjective, how do you conjugate a verb, etc.). He was the main reason I chose a degree in Biblical Languages rather than Theology.

Studying the Bible calmed my stormy seas and gave me a reason to get up in the morning, it awakened in me a hunger to know more, but also slowly made me realize that what I had been taught in church since I was thirteen years old might not in fact have been correct. By the time I graduated, I was left with more questions than answers, and I did not know how to proceed in my search or career. I couldn't teach college with just a bachelor's degree. And I couldn't find a master's degree I was interested in or one that I could afford.

Over the following year, I got married and worked at Macy's until one day, I was struck by the idea to contact the author of a book I had really enjoyed and ask him where I could study more about the Hebraic heritage of Christianity (the topic I was interested in, and which he specialized in). He wrote back to me; long story short, my beloved husband and I packed our bags and pets and moved down to Tulsa, Oklahoma.

A week before classes started, however, I dropped out of grad school because I was overcome with doubts about whether I would find the objective answers I sought there. Another year went by, and the pull to study the Bible returned once more. To end this tug of war, I decided to look for a middle ground and pursue an impartial career as a Bible translator. I reenrolled at the same school and signed up for a double master's degree in Advanced Biblical Languages and Judaic-Christian Studies.

Graduate school was no walk in the park. As someone who had only ever written two research papers in her life and was suddenly expected to start spitting one out in every class, my first semester was a trial by fire. And the only thing that got me through it was the frantic panic that I would crash and burn. But I didn't. And when I emerged on the other side, it was like seeing the Bible for the first time. I could no longer stomach the wishy-washy teachings in daily devotionals and run-of-the-mill sermons, which paled in comparison to the precious gold I had found. The type of pure gold you could only reach after reading the text in the original languages, comparing the variant readings, checking the lexicons for the usage of the words, combing through the commentaries, and consulting the primary sources.

The puzzle pieces in my mind were finally starting to fit together. But I was still uncertain about my career path. I had deserted the idea of being a Bible translator and was considering pursuing the heights of academia. Presenting at a single regional conference for the Society of Biblical Literature was enough for me to realize, however, that my place was not among scholars who treated the Bible as just another piece of ancient literature to be studied like a long-dead animal, poked, prodded, and dissected out of scientific curiosity. For me, it was a spring of living water, running deep through underground caverns and elaborate caves, beckoning to be discovered and explored.

During my last year of graduate school, I found a part-time job teaching Hebrew at a small Christian academy. A friend who had taught there was leaving, and they were looking for a replacement. It was an excellent experience to add to my resume, so I stayed there for three years and taught one yearbook class and one class about Jesus and his world. I thought I had finally found my place in the world during my first two years. I was able not only to teach (something I immensely enjoyed) but to teach subjects I was passionate about. I loved my students, and during my second year, I poured countless hours into my job, believing it would all be worth it. My students and I studied hard, but we also sang songs, played games, went to the Jewish museum, and made cookies with the Israeli emissary.

We are taught that hard work produces results, so if I taught well enough and spread the word far enough, I would have more work and more students the following year. But I did not receive recognition for my efforts, extra promotion of my classes was not allowed, new interest was not sparked, the number of my students remained insufficient to cover the cost of my classes, and at the start of my third year, I was almost not hired back to work.

Getting out of bed in the mornings began to take longer, lesson prep was shorter, the school hallways felt colder, and the time I spent with my students turned bitter-sweet. In my time off, I pursued every career avenue I could think of, other Christian high schools, Jewish-Christian relations, undergraduate Bible education, and even museum work. But nothing came out of it. By the time COVID hit in the spring of 2020, I had already seen the writing on the wall and was not at all surprised when I was informed that, regrettably, I wouldn't be rehired the following fall.

I had lost not only my job but my students and, worst of all, the opportunity to do what I had finally come to recognize as my calling, teaching Hebrew and the Bible. As I thought about my life, I imagined how bizarre and absurd it would seem to my teenage self that I would end up wanting to be a teacher. Maybe it happened because I am an enneagram type one, or maybe it was the difference that the teachers who had actually cared about me had made in my life, but there it was.

I was at a crossroads. I could do what I had done after college and apply for any job that would give me money. After all, all my efforts to progress in ANY of the career paths I had tried to pursue had produced zero results.

Or I could take a leap of faith and do the one last thing I had not tried. A thing for which I would need to use everything I had learned in the past (photography, lighting, art, design, research, writing, etc.) A thing that, in the end, might not work either. And despite my fear of complete and final failure, I decided to create my own classroom where I could teach what I wanted and however I wanted. I decided to create a YouTube channel.

Despite a college professor who discouraged me from pursuing a career as a bible scholar because I was a "lady" and would need time to take care of my family, and even though women bible scholars are few and far between, I chose to carve my own scholarly path in a way relevant to this generation, where I would take academic bible research and present it in a simple, straightforward manner, understandable to the average layperson.

I got to work and produced my first video...four months later! From the very start, obstacles popped up at every turn, not knowing a thing about video editing, needing to buy new equipment, falling and breaking my dominant arm while roller skating, my cat getting diabetes, worrying that my husband might lose his job, the extra stress causing my body to suffer, and on and on. Furthermore, I was living under the delusion that if I just figured out video editing and made that first video series, it would all just be rinse and repeat afterward.

When my first two videos did not become overnight hits, this impatient elder millennial sighed and grudgingly accepted that Rome had indeed not been built in a day. So, I dabbled in social media marketing, which worked but required funds I was short on. From the beginning, my plan also included having a website where I could receive donations and sell study materials. But creating a website without having the funds to pay someone to do it ended up posing a more significant challenge than learning video editing ever had. In short, I sobered up and faced the cold truth that just because I was trying to create a non-profit teaching ministry for the common good of humanity, I would not be able to get it off the ground without a lot more time and money.

But hope was not lost. Out of nowhere, a small group of strangers reached out to me, asking me to teach them modern

Hebrew. And then another few wanted to learn it online. That gave me the funds to purchase new equipment and video editing software. It also turned out that my brother could help me with the web design, but I would need to put in a lot of hours before I had a functioning website.

I am nowhere near being out of the woods yet, and who knows if I ever will be. I keep fighting to move forward a few inches at a time, even if that means crawling on scraped elbows and knees. My situation is far from ideal, but I choose to believe that if I am on the right path, I will make it through. I ignore the voice of fear and doubt in my head saying: "What if it doesn't work? What if you fail?" and instead put my trust in the LORD who says: "Fear not, for I am with you; be not dismayed, for I am your God. I will strengthen you, I will help you, I will uphold you with my righteous right hand." **Isaiah 41:10** (NKJV)

So, no matter what stage of your journey, don't get discouraged. Some of us travel slower than others and have to bang our heads in the dark many times before we get it right. What matters is that you keep going because if you are on the right path, God will part the waters and clear a way for you.

CONCLUSION
"WHEN THE SOLUTION IS SIMPLE, GOD IS ANSWERING." -ALBERT EINSTEIN

If you've been on this planet for any length of time, you know that life doesn't hold back any punches when it comes to challenges, adversity, and even downright injustice and trauma. If you don't know already, there are forces in this world that do not have your best intentions at heart!

Too many people blame God for the bad things that happen in their life, but the opposite is actually true. He (God) sent His Son, Jesus, not only to come into a relationship with us but so we can find true happiness and fulfillment through Him!

The Bible says in **John 10:10** (AMP), "The thief (Satan) comes only in order to steal and kill and destroy. I (Jesus) came that they may have and enjoy life, and have it in abundance [to the full, till it overflows]."

1 Peter 5:8-10 says, "Be sober, be vigilant; because your adversary the devil walks about like a roaring lion, seeking whom he may devour. Resist him, steadfast in the faith, knowing that the same sufferings are experienced by your brotherhood in the world. But may the God of all grace, who called us to His eternal glory by Jesus Christ, after you have suffered a while, perfect, establish, strengthen and settle you."

After everything I've been through in my life, I know that I wouldn't be here today if I didn't have a personal relationship with Jesus Christ. Now, that doesn't mean that all my problems disappear or that life will be a "bed of roses," but it does mean that we are able to have a relationship with the Creator of the universe and have peace that surpasses our human understanding. Also, He gives us the strength and additional tools to overcome whatever life throws at us and fulfill our purpose on the earth!

Jesus said in **John 14:27** (NLT), "I am leaving you with a gift – peace of mind and heart. And the peace I give is a gift the world cannot give. So don't be troubled or afraid."

I understand that the "God stuff" may resonate with some of you, and for others, it may not. But, for those whom it does not, I would like to thank you for supporting this project, this book, and for taking the time to read the stories we put together for you! Your life has a purpose! You Matter! And Your Story Matters too!

THE INVITATION

For those of you whom this "God stuff" does resonate with, I would like to share a bit more...

I received Jesus Christ into my life at a very young age. However, from the age of 15 into my early 20s, I lived a reckless life! I had strayed far from God, much like the story in the Bible of "The Prodigal Son." I had filled my life with things that were destroying it. Sex, drugs, and alcohol had brought me to the end of myself. It brought me to a place where I could have ended up dead or in prison. But, all the while, God was there, patiently waiting for me to return, just like the Prodigal Son returning to his Father.

There was a massive void in my life. No person, thing, experience, or money could ever fill. I recognized that the very thing I was searching for, to fill that void, was there all along. Jesus Christ had been continually knocking on the door of my heart, sending people across my path who would share specific things about God and who He is until finally, I gave my life to Him entirely. Emphasis on "Entirely!" I returned to Him and asked

Him to forgive my sins and deliver me from all the things that were trying to kill me!

From that day until now, my life has never been the same! No one can tell me or convince me that there isn't a God or that Jesus Christ can't turn our lives around entirely because I have experienced the love of God, peace, and grace that the world or anything in it can't provide. I am alive today because of it!

I believe that if you have read this far, what I am about to say is for you! I believe that God is knocking at the door of your heart! This is probably not the first time you've felt like He is. This confirms that Jesus is reaching out to you once again and inviting you into a personal relationship with Him! I realize that you may not understand it all, but the Good News is that you don't have to. It only requires simple faith. Here are a few more Bible verses that speak about having a relationship with God, the Creator of the universe, through His Son, Jesus Christ.

Revelation 3:20 says, "Behold, I stand at the door and knock. If anyone hears My voice and opens the door, I will come in to him and dine with him, and he with me."

John 1:12 says, "But as many as received Him, to them He gave the right to become children of God, to those who believe in His name."

Romans 10:9-10 says, "...if you confess with your mouth the Lord Jesus and believe in your heart that God has raised him from the dead, you will be saved. For with the heart one believes unto righteousness, and with the mouth confession is made unto salvation."

Romans 10:13 says, "...whoever calls on the name of the LORD shall be saved."

Ephesians 2:8-9 says, "For by grace you have been saved through faith, and that not of yourselves: it is the gift of God, not of works lest anyone should boast."

And finally, Jesus said in **John 14:6**, "...I am the way, the truth, and the life. No one comes to the Father except through Me."

So, it's really quite simple. It only requires simple faith; the Bible describes it as the faith of a child. If you would like to accept and receive Jesus Christ into your life as your Lord and Savior, you can do that today! Pray this simple prayer:

Prayer:

Father God, thank you for sending your Son, Jesus Christ, to die on the cross as a sacrifice, to forgive me of my sins so that I could enter into a relationship with you!

Jesus Christ, I believe that you are knocking at the door of my heart, and Your Word says that if I open the door of my heart to You and ask You to come in, You will. Your word also says that "whoever calls on the name of the Lord shall be saved."

Lord Jesus, I am asking you today to forgive me of my sins, come into my life, and become my Lord and Savior. Thank you for dying on the cross for me and rising from the dead on the third day so that I could also be raised into eternal life!

If you prayed that prayer, even with a simple, childlike faith, He has come into your life as your Lord and Savior! Get ready because you are going to start seeing things very differently.

1. The next best steps for you at this point would be to find a good Bible-based church in your area, ask God to show you, and He will.

2. Invest in a Bible; There are several different translations, but the one that helped me when I really started learning about God and the life of Jesus was the New Living Translation or NLT.

3. Start reading The Book of Proverbs, The Book of John, and The Book of Acts in the Bible.

Also, for a very powerful series on the life of Jesus, you can stream "The Chosen" series for free at:

https://watch.angelstudios.com/thechosen

ABOUT AARON JANDA

Aaron Janda is a 3x Amazon Best Selling Author, Publisher, Speaker, and Serial Entrepreneur. Aaron authored his first book, *My $100 Dollar Project*, a book that challenges readers to take $100 and multiply it to $1000 and beyond. Aaron co-authored his second book, *Influence and Income Online* that went Amazon #1 Best Seller in 5 categories. Aaron also co-authored the Best Selling Books, *Overcoming Adversity in Entrepreneurship,* and *The Kingdom Mind*. Aaron's recently released book, *Your Story Matters: Volume One* is the first in a six part book series sharing some of the most compelling and inspiring stories about overcoming trauma, overcoming adversity and finding hope to completely change your life!

Aaron has launched multiple 6-figure businesses, lost everything, and rebuilt his life and business' for the third time. He will be sharing more of his story in his upcoming book "Refuse To Quit." Aaron is passionate about helping others and sharing his story in hopes that it can help someone who is facing what may seem to be impossible circumstances.

Aaron is also the Founder of Legacy Publishing Co. A Publishing Company who's three core values are to:

1) Maximize the platform for Entrepreneurs, Influencers, and anyone else who wants to leave a lasting impact on the world through authorship.

2) Fund projects to help those who are not able to help themselves.

3) Create generational wealth to leave a lasting Legacy for generations to come. If you have a story to tell, Aaron would love to give you a free book consultation! He is also taking applications to be a contributor to the book series: *Your Story Matters*. Submit your information to https://www.legacypublishingco.com/contact

Aaron would love to help add value to your business or organization. If you would like to book Aaron to speak at your school or event, contact him for more info at the email below.

Scan with camera app for more Books, Courses & Coaching.

info@legacypublishingco.com
https://stan.store/aaronjanda

Made in the USA
Coppell, TX
02 October 2023